Praise for Pass

This book is a must-read for teachers who want to empower students to become self-sufficient lifelong learners. It is a guidebook for creating a vibrant classroom where student learning is the first priority.

—**Kristin Gomez, MA, director of orchestras at Jefferson Middle School and Abingdon Elementary School**

As an elementary student who was totally inspired by my elementary music teacher, I was so excited about this book, and it did not disappoint. As I watch my daughters grow up and be inspired by music in their lives, I read this thinking, *This is the type of music education I want for my own kids.* This is a great book that reminds us that music education should be in every school in the world. Thank you to the authors for sharing their experience and ideas with the world!

—**George Couros, educator and author of *The Innovator's Mindset***

Music teachers are often required to attend professional development that does not seem to relate to our performance-driven classes. We are left to figure out the applications on our own. *Pass the Baton* makes the connections for us in a way that empowers not only music students but music teachers. While it is easy to keep teaching the way we always have, it is exciting to think of giving our kids the skills to create, perform, respond, and connect in ways that let them explore their own curiosity and creativity.

—**Mari Schay, editor of *Activate!* Magazine and early elementary music teacher**

Pass the Baton is a must-read for all who desire to provide their students with access and opportunities to a lifetime of music-making and a deep love of music. As a veteran music educator, I am excited to implement many of the ideas found in this incredible resource! With an emphasis on the artistic processes of creating, performing, responding, and connecting, the authors have done an outstanding job at presenting concepts and connections to build a culturally responsive, relevant, and meaningful music education resource that is collaborative and student-centric. This comprehensive resource is filled with practical examples that every music educator can use right away to transform their teaching from simply engaging their students to offering every learner a voice and choice in their music education.

—Scott Sheehan, NAfME president-elect (2020–2022), music educator, and department chair, Hollidaysburg Area School District

In *Pass the Baton*, you will learn about what is possible when you shift the focus from engagement to empowerment. Theresa and Kathryn share inspiring examples and practical strategies for music education that apply to all of us as educators.

—Katie Martin, PhD, educator and author of *Learner-Centered Innovation*

Pass the Baton was an absolute joy to read from cover to cover. Over the course of its thirteen lively chapters, Kathryn and Theresa's duet offers a symphony of student-centered pedagogy with actionable strategies that play just as well outside of the music classroom as they do inside of it. As a school-based instructional coach, I found myself scribbling copious notes at each new coda and blatantly cribbing ideas with each chapter-ending encore. "If we stay where it's comfortable, we fall behind. Learning never stops." Brava, ladies! This book is sensational.

—John Meehan, high school instructional coach and author of *EDrenaline Rush*

Pass the Baton is the book music teachers have been looking for. As our education system shifts from engagement to empowerment, Kathryn and Theresa have provided the map for empowering our music students from kindergarten through twelfth grade. This is both a "why" and a "how" book. Each chapter explains a different aspect of empowerment, lists practical tips, and shows real-life examples of teachers who integrate the book's strategies in their own music rooms. Kathryn and Theresa have provided a practical blueprint for shifting from engagement to empowerment in music education. They tackle the logistical issues of how to incorporate choice and boost student agency while also covering the standards and promoting skill development. Along the way, they share inspiring stories and relevant insights. This is a must-read for anyone interested in helping music students own their learning.

—Dr. John Spencer, professor and author

Theresa and Kathryn have laid out a thoughtful and accessible model for facilitating empowered musical education and enlightenment. For those of us who have been in the business for an age, and for those who are recently joining the conversation, this book clarifies the multiple processes of classroom music/instrumental education. The clarity of thought and unrelenting focus on the concept of empowerment is profound and will foment a self-sustaining circle of success.

—Denny Stokes, founding conductor, Virginia Winds Academy, and conductor, George Mason University Symphonic Band

Pass the Baton is the perfect adaptable resource we have needed in music education! Kathryn Finch and Theresa Hoover have achieved the ideal balance of thought-provoking, accessible guidance and practical resources and activities. Music educators looking to facilitate their students having more autonomy, buy-in, and voice need to check out this book! We need to take a step back so our students can take a step forward; this book gives us the tools to do so!

—Scott N. Edgar, PhD, associate professor of music, Lake Forest College, author of *Music Education and Social Emotional Learning: The Heart of Teaching Music*

In my last ten years of teaching internationally, I've heard over and over that the "traditional band class is irrelevant to today's students." While there is some truth to that statement, what is more important is that the traditional methods of teaching band do not resonate with many students. *Pass the Baton* offers tested and practical teaching methods relevant to current students, engaging them, empowering them, and reinvigorating your program to bring new glories beyond the traditional awards and performances.

—Mandy Hollingshead, international music educator

I read this, thinking, *This is* Shift This! *written specifically to benefit our students of music!* Music educators can learn from Kathryn and Theresa's experience with student voice, choice, and student-directed learning, which leads to empowerment and confidence in our students, develops leadership and learning *beyond* the school building. The authors supplement their "why" with specific examples and ideas music educators can use the very next day, paving the way for students to become lifelong makers of music.

—Joy Kirr, educator and author of *Shift This!*

What an inspiring, motivating, and *empowering* resource that offers numerous innovative and immediately implementable ideas for music classrooms with students of any age and discipline. The authors draw upon their combined decades of teaching successes and challenges to illustrate the importance of shaking ourselves out of our comfort zones while affording students creative, lasting, and impactful opportunities to take ownership of their musical growth. The authors weave together a wealth of resources, practical strategies, current technologies, and "shovel-ready" initiatives that will undoubtedly empower any teacher to pass the baton.

—Ryan Nowlin, coauthor, *Tradition of Excellence*
Comprehensive Band Method

I highly recommend this book for all music educators, from those in their first year of teaching to the more experienced. It's full of great ideas about creative paths for developing critical thinkers and listeners in music at all levels.

—Linda Gammon, Virginia Winds Academy, junior winds conductor

In *Pass the Baton*, Kathryn Finch and Theresa Hoover offer a well-organized battle plan for empowering students in music education classes and ensembles. The "empowered music student" has a voice and a choice, creates and consumes, asks questions, is connected, and exhibits ownership in the process. The agency for which Finch and Hoover advocate makes music learning more engaging and students more motivated. Each chapter moves thoughtfully from an accessible presentation of pedagogical philosophy to actionable application. *Pass the Baton* is a welcome book on a timely topic by two passionate and gifted music educators—highly recommended!

—Dr. Scott Watson, composer and music educator

As a principal who is also a musician, I often work to translate new educational ideas and PD for my music teachers. This book takes so many current educational best practices and connects them directly to day-to-day work being done by my music teachers. I cannot wait to share it with them! Hoover and Finch have done the music world a huge service in writing this book. For the first time, I have read a book filled with so many great insights and ways to maximize instructional time by switching the focus of instruction from teacher-centered to student-centered. All music educators can benefit from this book— and their administrators can learn how to design and evaluate great instruction in a music classroom!

—Dr. Matt Sieloff, middle school principal

Pass the Baton

Pass the Baton

Empowering All Music Students

by Kathryn Finch and Theresa Hoover

Pass the Baton: Empowering All Music Students
© 2020 Kathryn Finch and Theresa Hoover

This book is available at special discounts when purchased in quantity for educational purposes or as premiums, promotions, or fundraisers. For inquiries and details, contact the publisher at books@daveburgessconsulting.com.

Published by Dave Burgess Consulting, Inc.
San Diego, CA
DaveBurgessConsulting.com

Library of Congress Control Number: 2020944792
Paperback ISBN: 978-1-951600-54-9
Ebook ISBN: 978-1-951600-55-6

Cover design by Michael Miller
Interior design by Liz Schreiter
Editing and production by Reading List Editorial: readinglisteditorial.com

To the students, for opening our eyes, pushing our thinking, and continuing to surprise us regularly. May you always have music in your lives.
—Theresa

To Andrew, Hope, and Christopher for supporting me following a dream and for loving me unconditionally. May you follow your own dreams and believe you can do hard things.
—Kathryn

Contents

Foreword

Class began that day with a heightened sense of excitement and anticipation. Students took their seats as usual, with instruments and music in hand, but they also held unique research reports they had completed. Curtis stood up first to share his idea for the new composition. Other students jotted down notes and applauded when he concluded. Then it was Sierra's turn. As she stood up to face the band, you could sense the deep reverence she had for her topic.

She said, "I believe the composition should be based on Georgia O'Keeffe. She is one of the most important women in American history." After a brief pause, and filled with more emotion, Sierra continued: "She is from our town and is very important to all of us. Her story shows her determination to live out a dream even when it had been ripped away. She showed that we can all achieve our goals even if we have to change the path we take." The moment was stunning. Everyone in the room saw a bit of themselves in the story Sierra told about our Sun Prairie native. The students quickly found consensus as we submitted our idea to the composer.

Eleven years ago, I posed an audacious question to my middle school band: "If we were to commission a composer to write a piece of music for us, what would the piece be about and why?" Sierra's suggestion was one of many imaginative and creative ideas we considered. Through collaboration with nationally renowned composer Samuel R. Hazo, the class decided to create a sonic representation of O'Keeffe's painting *Blue and Green Music.* My students dove into the project with zeal, researching O'Keeffe, the painting, and her connection to our city. Our mayor, who is an O'Keeffe expert, joined the ensemble on a tour of local historic sites on our way to the Milwaukee Art Museum to see O'Keeffe paintings and a music clinic at the UW–Milwaukee. The world-premiere performance took place at the Wisconsin State Music Conference with the composer conducting.

Just before the performance, the composer commented: "I always love coming to Patrick Marsh Middle School. They don't chase down the notes—they chase down everything that has to do with the music. In fact, they know the piece better than I know the piece, and I wrote it." The performance included the story of our creative journey as told by the students themselves. Making the day even more extraordinary, members of Georgia O'Keeffe's family sat in the front row. After our performance, I looked at the O'Keeffe family's faces as they sat arm in arm with tears in their eyes. The middle school band, understanding the significance of the moment, did not want to leave the stage.

Through this lesson, we created a climate of possibility, allowing students to act upon their curiosity and to explore their imagination while empowering them to create something with meaning that transcended their own lives. Through intentional planning, students were at the origins of creativity, interacting with composers, artists, historians, and community members. Without question, this was one of the most meaningful teaching experiences of my life, and it all started with trusting and empowering my students.

I hadn't always taught like this. I had tried unsuccessfully to do the "command and control" bit from the podium. After just a few years of teaching, I was burned out and looking for another career. When I started empowering my students, recognizing the curiosity and passion within them, I noticed that my students achieved more and enjoyed the class more.

Let's face it: teaching is complex and challenging work. No two classes or students are the same. A standardized, top-down approach will never work. We must realize that inside each of our students is a beautiful narrative yet to unfold. Our job is to nurture this potential by creating an environment that cultivates growth—an environment that recognizes that each of our students has something to add. If we want them to make good decisions moving forward, then we need to create opportunities for students to make decisions.

This book beautifully illuminates the philosophy and process of empowering students. Theresa and Kathryn break down not only the "why" of empowerment but also the "how." Written by teachers for teachers, the pages that follow contain tested ideas and strategies that live within the authors' own classrooms. What's more, the book provides you with inspiring quotes, meaningful stories, uplifting ideas, creative strategies, amazing resources, and a good bit of humor as well!

I'm thrilled that you will have the opportunity to learn from Theresa and Kathryn. Enjoy the book and begin your journey to empowering your students!

—Chris Gleason

Instrumental music educator, Sun Prairie, WI

2017 Wisconsin Teacher of the Year

chrispgleason.com

Introduction

We know the power of music. As music educators, we have been impacted by our art. We have performed, created, and studied for countless hours, having made the decision to share our passion with children. We want only the best for our students, so that they too can have the same profound musical experiences we have had. This book evolved from that desire.

What you will find in this book are ideas, suggestions, and, most importantly, encouragement—encouragement to try something new, take a risk, and see what happens. If you want to change your music program, empower your students, and create a more learner-centered environment, then this book is for you. We hope it gives you guidance on where to start and the courage to take the plunge. If you're content with everything happening in your music program and just picked up this book for fun, it's still for you! We hope it inspires you to experiment and try new approaches with your students.

We love teaching, but over the years we felt something was missing in our instruction. Before delving into what that missing piece was, and how you can implement it in your classroom, we first want to introduce ourselves.

Theresa

My teaching career began in 2003 after I earned a bachelor's degree in music education from Penn State University. I taught for fourteen years in Pennsylvania, in a variety of settings, and also earned a master's degree in instrumental wind conducting from West Chester University. A move in 2016 brought me to Northern Virginia, where I got a job teaching fourth- and fifth-grade band and orchestra in a public elementary school just outside Washington, DC. The school is unique in that all students in those grades must participate in the band or orchestra and sing in the chorus! Both the instrumental and vocal music ensemble rehearsals take place during the school day. The band and orchestra small-group lessons, however, are on a pull-out rotation, where the students come out of their academic classrooms. They attend a thirty-minute group instrumental music lesson each week and a forty-five-minute ensemble rehearsal. All students attend a forty-five-minute general music class and forty-five-minute full chorus (the entire grade) rehearsal.

Since then, I've changed positions and currently teach sixth-through eighth-grade band and guitar in the same county. That school is on a block schedule where each class meets for eighty-three minutes every other day. I now teach about 125 students. In both schools, students have 1:1 iPads, which they use throughout the school day. I've been able to transfer many of the shifts I made in the elementary school setting to the middle school.

At one time my classroom was very teacher led. I worked hard to have my band room function similarly to how the band rooms of my past did, working to emulate the conductors I'd played under in grade school and college. My students were compliant, and we made great music together. It was the move to Northern Virginia that helped me realize something was missing. My new school was offering optional summer professional-development workshops, and, having just moved to the area, I figured it might be a good idea to attend. A session about flipped classroom techniques blew my mind! I discovered that the tra-ditional way of teaching—from the front of the room with students quietly listening—wasn't the only way. And it might not be the most effective way either! While flipped classroom techniques are just one of the many ideas I have explored, I understand now that quiet does not equal learning. On task doesn't equal learning either. Students who own the music-making process—that equals learning!

Kathryn

I'm a K–5 general music teacher with twenty-plus years of experience in the classroom. I studied at Augustana College, where I received my bachelor's degree in music education and studied voice. A few years later, I returned to graduate school for my master's degree in music education at VanderCook College of Music and obtained all three levels of the Orff Schulwerk certification. I teach in an elementary school in a northern suburb of Chicago and see all grade levels two times a week for half an hour. I teach the entire school population, about 430 students. All students participate in one school performance each year. Kindergarten has an informance (informational performance) in the music classroom in March, first through fourth graders take part in a Winter Sing in December, and fifth graders participate in a musical in May. Students can join the orchestra in third grade and the band in fourth. They all have their own iPads as a result of a recent 1:1 district initiative. I have my own classroom and work with a team of music educators in the district that meets monthly.

I also spent many years keeping a compliant, teacher-led classroom. It was a very engaging place to be. My principal often told me students loved my lessons and were excited to see what I would do next—however, I didn't know what the students were taking away from these experiences. I didn't always check for understanding, nor did I give students enough credit.

For example, one time a student shared a composition he had created on his own at home. Amazed, I asked, "How did you learn to do that?" He looked at me funny and said, "You taught me." He'd clearly pulled together all the skills I had taught the class and created a composition at home, but I was shocked at his product.

I didn't like that I was so surprised. I realized I should have *all* my students composing, creating, and applying new skills to projects that mean something to *them*. The student who shared his composition was beaming with enthusiasm. Why should he be the only one to have this experience? This is when I realized I needed to make some changes. I had to do things differently.

♫

We were both successful teachers, helping students enjoy making music, but we both realized something was missing. When we met in 2017 on Twitter, which we'll go into more detail about later, we were able to discuss that missing element and work together to make changes in our classrooms. Once we connected and exchanged ideas, we felt we had to share them with other teachers.

Throughout this book, we will talk about our experiences in the classroom and what worked for our situations. It's then up to you, dear reader, to determine how to make things work for your students. Every music room is unique, and every music teacher is an individual. What worked for us may not work precisely the same way for you. Start with small shifts, use trial and error, and go from there. We also want you to know we are writing from experience, and, while we have read and will quote others' research, we base this book on our years of teaching and our journey toward innovation in music education.

We would never suggest that our current methods are the best or preferred over any other—but they've worked successfully for us, and we hope they will for you as well.

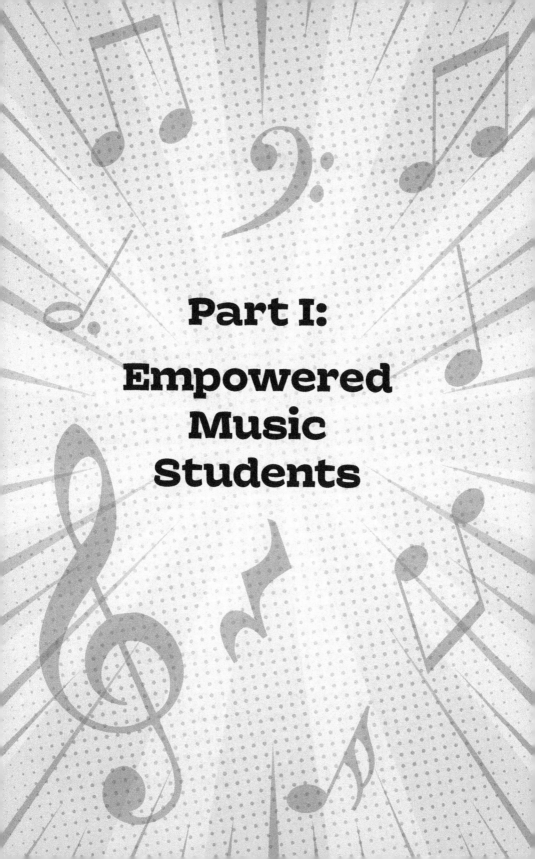

Part I:

Empowered Music Students

1

It Starts with You

So often we worry about what we can't do or what we don't have control over. Usually our schedules are planned and created for us by administrators. Many of us have no control over the size of our ensembles or what time of day they rehearse. Performances are predetermined, and the amount of planning time we get is beyond our control. Sometimes it feels like there are too many constraints in our way for us to make meaningful change. However, we encourage you to think about what you *can* do. *You* run rehearsals day after day. *You* build relationships with students. *You* create the culture inside the classroom. There is power in your classroom and in your instruction. Use it. It starts with you.

Where to Begin

Before venturing on this journey, take some time to think about your goals for your music students and for your music program. What is your mission statement? What do you want your students to know and be able to do when they leave your program? This will most likely be different for each of us, but we imagine that somewhere at the core, everyone wants their students to be lifelong learners of music. We don't expect them all to major in music or to become professional musicians. Instead, we hope they'll find opportunities to create their own music and consume it in their daily lives. We hope they will grow into adults who consider singing in the church choir or playing in a community band or orchestra. They will be parents who sing to their children and encourage participation in musical activities. They will become school board members who fight for music programs when others threaten to make cuts. They will fondly look back at their time in the school music program and recognize its importance, its value, and the impact it made on their lives.

As music teachers, we challenge everyone in our profession to push their thinking and to never stop reflecting on their programs and instruction. We owe that to our students. As educators, we have to stay relevant to them and provide a culture that listens and responds to their needs. We can make a change by giving students ownership, considering their needs first, and empowering them as musicians. That would be life changing.

Scaffolding

Scaffolding will be necessary throughout this process. You will need to provide levels of temporary support as students move toward independence. New information will need to be delivered in small chunks, and routines should be developed so expectations are clear. The supports can be removed incrementally as students progress and no longer need them. If you have a very traditional classroom in a very traditional school, you'll have to shift instruction gradually to a more student-led experience. Take your time. Make one small shift to begin with, and only make additional shifts when your students have shown they are ready. Don't get ahead of yourself. It's a marathon, not a sprint.

This process will also require you to repeatedly reflect. If the shift was a flop, why? What happened? We all make mistakes. What's great about those experiences is the feedback we receive. What do we keep working on so next time is better? This is a great opportunity to model for our students how to reflect, persevere, and try again. Don't be afraid to ask them their opinions. What you might consider a flop may have been a win for them!

Be prepared to find that not all of your students will be at the same place at the same time—that would be too easy. Some students will arrive with more experience than others, and therefore they may have different comfort levels. The idea is to meet them where they are. Help each learner get from his or her point A to point B. You will notice throughout this book many strategies offer flexibility. Embrace this!

Modeling

As the teacher, you'll need to model what you want from your students. If you want them to be creative self-starters who will take a risk and reflect on the process, then you too must push your thinking and have a growth mindset to learn new things. It's okay and important to share your mistakes and failures with your students. Show how you learned from them and how "fail" doesn't have to be a bad word. Instead, it's feedback that pushes thinking forward.

If your students see you as a lifelong learner, it will be easier for them to see themselves that way too. Model growth. They should also see you as a lifelong musician! It's amazing to us when some students are surprised to hear that we actually play music in addition to teaching it. If you perform outside of school and it's appropriate, invite your students! If the venue isn't student friendly, consider showing them a video instead. Our students love seeing videos of us as performers. It makes being a musician seem more real and attainable.

The next time you share accomplishments from a famous composer, consider taking a different approach. Instead of only sharing their great accomplishments, share their failures along the way. Do composers have to overcome hardships and failures before they succeed? Rachmaninoff's debut of his Symphony No. 1 in D minor received such poor reviews that it sent him into a depressive state and stopped him from composing for a few years. However, he was able to move past this setback and compose Piano Concerto No. 2 in C minor, one of his most popular works. Composer Jennifer Jolley has an entire Instagram page and blog (whycompose.com) dedicated to her rejection letters! Everyone hits bumps along the road; it's part of the process. How you pick up the pieces and push forward is what's important.

Building Relationships

It will come up time and time again in this book, but building relationships with your students is vital. As you shift to empowering them, you will find that it requires a certain level of trust. Music teachers will have to trust their students and vice versa. It's only when this trust has been built that the shift from teacher-directed to student-led learning can occur.

For a music teacher, this can be a challenge because of the number of students you see in a week. Make the effort anyway. Use their names frequently. Smile and say hello in the hallway. Ask about their weekends, after-school activities, or hobbies. So much value and power lies in knowing our students well and beginning to focus our instruction on their likes and needs. When they feel cared for and actively part of a classroom, they thrive. Share about yourself, within reason. Tell them about your interests and hobbies. As mentioned before, share about yourself as a musician. This is how we build trust and model a growth mindset.

Part of our job is to help students see themselves as creative, musical beings. They have something important to say, and not every child inherently

> **Part of our job is to help students see themselves as creative, musical beings.**

knows this. Getting to know students is never a waste of time. Use the conversations you have with them to build on the learning they're experiencing. For some students, words won't be enough. They will be angry or hurt and won't believe your words. For these students, your actions will have more effect. What matters is what you do for them. Ask them to help before or after class with a special task, or make an effort to attend one of their activities after school.

Other students will notice what you did for one of their classmates: how you made an adaptive recorder for a child without breath support or spent the time to find a valuable musical task for a friend of theirs who broke his arm and couldn't play the ukulele during music class. Every empathetic moment you spend with your students will be rewarding and powerful. It sends the message that in your classroom they are cared for and are to care for others. Sadly, these moments often don't happen enough, so when you make the effort, it will be noticed and valued.

Learning is social and collaborative. It does not take place in a vacuum. As a result, students will have to trust one another. Allow opportunities for them to build relationships with their classmates and fellow musicians. Taking a cue from social-emotional learning (SEL) strategies, model and practice working collaboratively, giving and receiving feedback, and other skills they will encounter in the music classroom. Help students make the music room the safe place we know it should be.

Before moving into the next sections of this book, take a minute to think about your music room and your music classes:

> ♪ What are your goals for your students?
> ♪ What do you want them to gain from their time with you?
> ♪ What do you want them to ultimately remember and take away?

Write your answers down somewhere so you can refer back to them often. Knowing and believing in these goals will guide you as you begin your journey.

2

What Does It Mean to Be Empowered?

Students singing, playing instruments, composing, listening to and evaluating music . . . these are all examples of them being engaged in music. Students are active participants in the music classroom. As teachers, many of us want this. In fact, we take great pride in making music joyful and engaging. Music educators reach much of a school's population. Music is a place for all. And yet, is engagement enough?

Another way to look at this is through a typical school ensemble performance: the conductor chose the music, studied the score, prepared for and led rehearsals, conducted the performance, and took a bow at the end. In that scenario, who was making musical choices? Who had ownership over the music-making process? Most likely, it was not the performers. The conductor made musical choices and gave the piece expressive value. However, if we want our students to become musicians, why are we not giving them these same opportunities?

What if, instead of merely engaging our students, we empowered them to take part in choosing repertoire, listening and reflecting on their own work, and offering feedback to their peers? What if they could not only participate in making music but also *own* the process? Wouldn't this be more powerful?

Engagement vs. Empowerment

According to Oxford Dictionaries, to *engage* is to "occupy or attract (someone's interest or attention)." To *empower* is to "give (someone) the authority or the power to do something" or to "make (someone) stronger or more confident, especially in controlling their life and claiming their rights." When you put it that way, shouldn't we want empowered students?

Bill Ferriter explains the difference between engaged students and empowered students in this image:

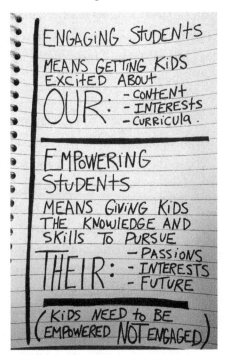

Engaged vs. empowered students. William M. Ferriter,
https://www.flickr.com/photos/plugusin/12188008225/.

In both cases, the students are excited about learning and are most likely active participants. The difference is in who drives the learning. Is it the teacher or the student? In terms of music students, think about this:

Engaged music students:

- ♪ sing or play music chosen by the teacher
- ♪ listen and move to music selected by the teacher
- ♪ learn about composers the teacher feels are important
- ♪ create music within guidelines and for purposes expressed by the teacher
- ♪ perform for events coordinated by the teacher
- ♪ follow a curriculum or learning path set by the teacher

Empowered music students:

- ♪ have a choice in the music they learn to sing, play, listen, and move to
- ♪ learn about composers they are curious about, maybe those who are from the same culture or racial background, are LGBTQ, or write a style of music that interests them
- ♪ compose and create music for a purpose important to them, such as for a friend or family member, about a story they enjoy, or for a special occasion
- ♪ help coordinate performances, either by choosing the event, having a choice in the music performed, writing song introductions, or decorating
- ♪ have a voice in their learning paths

When we as *teachers* are the driving force in the classroom, students react to what we put in front of them. Some will comply because that's what we taught them to do. Other students may become disconnected and disengage from these lessons. A few may become quiet and passive, while others act out with unwanted behaviors. Some may even be frustrated or angry. Often, as music educators, we get disheartened by students who don't want to comply with what we think is a fun, engaging lesson. But these behaviors tell us that something isn't right for those learners.

> **When you empower students, the focus shifts. Students become the driving force.**

When you empower students, the focus shifts. *Students* become the driving force, making learning more personal, meaningful, and powerful. They have a voice and a choice in their learning, and they have the creative freedom to make something that is their own. They see themselves as part of something bigger.

We've Come So Far

In the United States, the original focus for education was religion. Children were taught to read so they could understand Scripture. Eventually, writing and arithmetic were added to schooling, as was the focus on vocational training and higher education. To succeed in school, only compliance was necessary, and the same was true for many jobs. Citizens needed to follow instructions. School desks were in rows, with the teacher lecturing at the front of the room. Workers mindlessly punched time clocks, performing the same menial tasks day after day. Fast-forward to the twenty-first century, and this model is no longer relevant. Robots have replaced factory workers. More Americans than ever are self-employed, and that number is only expected to rise.

As technology advances, people must be able to adapt along with it. Schools have realized that they too must evolve so students can keep up with the ever-changing world, become lifelong learners, and compete in a global economy.[1] We can't keep doing the same thing and hope for different results. Project based learning, the 4 Cs (critical thinking, communication, collaboration, and creativity), and personalized learning are no longer a wish for public education but a necessity to ensure our students are future ready.

Music education in the schools has an origin story that is now equally irrelevant. When music schools began, the purpose was to help children improve their singing of religious music. Hymns were the primary source for music instruction. As music entered the public school system in the mid-to-late 1800s, the focus was still on instruction in performance and music theory—having the ability to read from hymnals.[2]

In 1950, MENC (Music Educators National Conference, now NAfME, the National Association for Music Education) published "The Child's Bill of Rights in Music," stating that all children have the right to a music education in school. This Bill of Rights later became the 1994 Music Education Standards.[3] While there was value in these standards—students singing, playing instruments, composing, improvising, etc.—the result was still only students who were engaged in music-making dictated by the music teacher. Luckily, NAfME updated the music standards in 2014, and they have now become the Core Music Standards. As a result, changes in instruction are slowly occurring. These changes better reflect the need for students to think critically, solve problems, and become well-rounded citizens.

Bob Phillips, a music educator, conductor, and the director of string publications for Alfred Music, asks, "Am I preparing kids for my past or their future?" That's an excellent question! Are we teaching our music students the same way we were taught? Are we teaching the way we want to be taught? Or are we teaching them the way they need (and want) to be taught? Our past differs greatly from their future.[4]

NAfME Core Music Standards

The NAfME Core Music Standards, as part of the National Core Arts Standards, focus on students having a more significant role in the music-making process. The standards include the following strands:

> ♪ Creating
> ♪ Performing
> ♪ Responding
> ♪ Connecting

1994 National Standards for Arts Education	2014 National Core Arts Standards
1. Singing, alone and with others, a varied repertoire of music. 2. Performing on instruments, alone and with others, a varied repertoire of music. 3. Improvising melodies, variations, and accompaniments. 4. Composing and arranging music within specified guidelines. 5. Reading and notating music. 6. Listening to, analyzing, and describing music. 7. Evaluating music and music performances. 8. Understanding relationships between music, the other arts, and disciplines outside the arts. 9. Understanding music in relation to history and culture. *From National Standards for Arts Education. Copyright © 1994 by Music Educators National Conference (MENC). Used by permission. The complete National Arts Standards and additional materials relating to the Standards are available from the National Association for Music Education, 1806 Robert Fulton Drive, Reston, VA 20191; nafme.org.*	**Creating** 1. Generate and conceptualize artistic ideas and work. 2. Organize and develop artistic ideas and work. 3. Refine and complete artistic work. **Performing/Presenting/ Producing** 4. Select, analyze, and interpret artistic work for presentation. 5. Develop and refine artistic techniques and work for presentation. 6. Convey meaning through the presentation of artistic work. **Responding** 7. Perceive and analyze artistic work. 8. Interpret intent and meaning in artistic work. 9. Apply criteria to evaluate artistic work. **Connecting** 10. Synthesize and relate knowledge and personal experiences to make art. 11. Relate artistic ideas and works with societal, cultural and historical context to deepen understanding. *National Core Arts Standards © 2015 National Coalition for Core Arts Standards. Rights administered by State Education Agency Directors of Arts Education (SEADAE). All rights reserved. nationalartsstandards.org*

While some aspects of the 2014 standards may seem similar to the 1994 standards, such as creating and performing, students are now much more involved in the learning process. Previously, they were required to sing, play, create, listen, and evaluate. Now they must interpret, apply, synthesize, develop, and refine artistic techniques as well. When creating, students begin by generating ideas, then plan and execute their creation, reflect on and refine their work, and finally present it to an audience. When performing, they first select, analyze, and interpret the work. Then they rehearse, evaluate, and refine it before presenting it to an audience. This differs from the typical scenario, where the teacher completes most tasks, and the students are only (somewhat) responsible for the final step, presenting.

Before worrying about the complexity involved in implementing the 2014 standards, understand that each step is modified to suit the needs of the learners. The extent to which a first-grade student will analyze and interpret a piece of music is much different from how an eighth-grade student will do it. As educators, we can scaffold the standards so the students reach these rigorous goals. No more should we teach individual skills in isolation. Instead, we must provide opportunities to create, perform, respond, and connect so students can experience the full music-making process.

When students are empowered, they own this process by taking responsibility for the planning, creating, refining, and presenting of their musical product. They select their own repertoire for performance and evaluation. And they connect music to their personal experiences and daily lives. With this, they can truly become musical. As educators, we are there to provide support and guidance so they can make appropriate musical choices. How will they learn if we never give them opportunities to try things on their own?

3

Why Should Music Students Be Empowered?

Why should we empower music students? It's simple. Think about your primary goal for your students. Is it to receive a "one" or "superior" at a festival? To give a flawless performance? Or is the goal for them to be musical and to become lifelong learners and lovers of music? If your goal is a perfect concert, we cannot help you. But if your desire has anything to do with your students being *musicians*, that's why you work to empower them—and that's what we hope this book will help you to do. After asking several music teachers their personal goals for their students, we received a variety of responses:

> That they will have positive experiences that encourage a lifetime of musical growth and enjoyment.
>
> —Brittany Brandt,
> general music teacher

My goal is for them to enjoy making music and to understand that anyone can make music.

—Giovanna Davilla, general music teacher

My wish for students when they leave my music classroom
is for them to know music is not for a chosen few who
decide to pursue playing an instrument or sing in a choir. I
want them to know creating, exploring, playing, analyzing,
and listening to music is for everyone.

—Kelly Harper, middle school general
music and choral director

I want to create musically literate students. I am such a
small part of their musical experience. Having the gift of
musical literacy means that music can be in their lives after
our time together is over.

—Nick Juknelis, high school choral director

Someone once told Theresa, "I was a music major in high school and
had four periods of music a day, but in none of them were we permitted
to make our own music. I got yelled at for tuning my own guitar, even
though I had been playing for ten years at the time." It made Theresa
think, *Is this what I want for my students? To never create music?* It definitely is not. Imagine if someone had empowered this student—her
musical growth would have increased exponentially! She could have
practiced music that was interesting and challenging to her. She could
have composed and even performed her own music. She could have
worked with classmates to teach, inspire, and collaborate. Instead, it
sounds like there were many missed opportunities.

Empower your music students so they don't miss opportunities.
Empower them so they develop a love for music and music-making.
Empower them to help them become amazing human beings.

We want our students to consume and create music for a lifetime. And
yet we won't always be there to lead them through an exercise in a book,
help them tune their instruments, or greet them with a fun, engaging

Empower them so they develop a love for music and music-making.

singing game. We want them to seek their own musical interests and perform, create, and consume music that brings them joy. It's exciting when students share music they learned outside of school. In a world with technology at students' fingertips, they don't have to wait for us to show them how to do something. They can explore and find answers on their own. They need us in a different way. After we've helped them self-reflect and create their own next steps, we can step back and let them have some of the control.

A Closer Look at Motivation

Kathryn: The biggest shift for me was learning what motivates students. Engaging lessons weren't always working anymore. Students were participating in class, but they didn't seem connected to the music-making. It was discouraging and baffling. Once I understood the science behind extrinsic and intrinsic motivation, I started to see how I could shift my instruction to boost engagement and empowerment in the classroom. When students are extrinsically motivated, they complete a task only to receive a reward. With intrinsic motivation, students complete the task because it matters to them. With gradual changes in my instruction, and a focus on intrinsic motivation, the excitement of learning and creating music was attainable again.

In his book *Drive*, Daniel Pink states that intrinsic motivation is much more powerful than extrinsic motivation. In fact, he argues that "carrots and sticks can promote bad behavior, create addiction, and encourage short-term thinking at the expense of the long view." What people—teachers and students alike—need for intrinsic motivation is autonomy, mastery, and purpose. When someone has autonomy, they have a choice. Choice over what to do, how to do it, and with whom to work. The pursuit of mastery comes from a desire to improve. Tasks must therefore be appropriately challenging, and people must believe they can improve and understand it will take perseverance. Purpose is the final requirement for intrinsic motivation. People must believe what they are doing has meaning and value.[1]

When students are engaged in music-making, the motivation is often extrinsic. The teacher ultimately has the autonomy, choosing what the students will learn. Students may or may not desire mastery of the skills being taught. They may not believe they can improve, or see value in the work that would be required to improve. While the teacher understands the purpose of the various musical activities, it may not be clear or relevant to the students. We can empower those students to find their own autonomy, mastery, and purpose. Instruction is not just given to them. They grapple with the learning, decide their next steps, and move to push their thinking forward.

How Will This Affect My Students?

Theresa: The most significant shift for me happened when I stopped asking, "How will this affect my [band] program?" and asked, "How will this affect my students?" *How will this help my students grow as musicians? How will this help learners develop a love for music-making? How will this help my students become lifelong musicians?* The center of our decision-making should be the learner. How will a decision benefit students and their journey to becoming musical?

In a social media group for music teachers, a member posted about being upset that his school was considering adding an orchestra program when there was already a successful band program in place. He was concerned about the negative impact it would have on his band program. There is validity to that thought process. Some students might participate in the orchestra instead of the band, decreasing enrollment in band. This change might affect the music they play, or the level at which they can achieve.

In situations like this, sometimes we don't recognize the potential positive impacts to the school's music program or the individual students. It could be an opportunity to give more students a musical outlet in school and have more musical experiences. Adding an orchestra program could give musicians the chance to experience different repertoire and different performances. It's natural to worry about our programs, but when we focus on our learners and their musical experiences, we can see new possibilities. It's not about us. It's about them. It's not our program. It's theirs. We are guides in their musical journey.

Theresa: A first-year violin student approached me about wanting to perform at an informal school event. She wanted to play "The Pink Panther." When she mentioned this piece, I paused—they were still working on the D-major scale in class. "The Pink Panther," with all its chromaticism, was much more complicated than that! I responded, "Oh! That's a tricky song!" And paused again. Before I continued my thought that maybe she should consider a different song, the student piped up with "Oh, that's okay, I learned it last night on YouTube!" And sure enough, she had! It wasn't perfect, but it was pretty darn good considering she learned it on her own. That is an empowered student. She didn't wait for me to teach her something that interested her. She took it upon herself and owned it! Can you imagine if I had told her no? I would have quashed her enthusiasm. Instead, this student taught herself something she was excited to learn and brought her enthusiasm to school to share her learning with others. Every student should have this opportunity.

Hidden Benefits

Some hidden benefits occurred along the way in the process of empowering our music students. Being absent and preparing substitute plans has become much easier! In the past, we worried that even if the sub was a musician, there was no way class could go on without us. And if the sub was not a musician, why bother? Now, with students taking ownership of their learning (and, therefore, the class), it's not difficult at all. While this might not work the first few weeks of school, once they get accustomed to it, students will understand how to self-motivate. We leave the substitute a list of activities our students should do, with instructions to select a different student to lead each activity. Empowered students will have already done this many times with you. It's no different with a sub!

Another unplanned benefit Theresa discovered when teaching elementary instrumental music was that more students continued in band and orchestra in middle school. When she set out to empower her students, one goal was for them to become lifelong learners and musicians. We have noticed that since she changed her approach in the classroom, empowering her students, more continue playing after the class is through! Upon consideration, it makes sense. When students own their music-making, it becomes more important to them. It becomes a part of them. It's only natural that they should want to keep doing it. We can't complain!

While this book is not about classroom management (in fact, we suggest that you already have control of your classroom before trying many of the strategies described here), another thing we have noticed is that behavior problems decrease when students feel ownership over their learning. They are more likely to be on task. They are less likely to disrupt the class because they see meaning in what they're doing and want to be a part of something bigger than themselves.

We recently witnessed an interaction between two students in a fifth-grade band lesson. One student, J, who was typically very outspoken and off task, spent nearly an entire class period working with and helping a classmate. The boys were more focused and worked independently longer than we'd ever seen from them before! Because they had chosen to work together and were clearly invested in their learning, J saw purpose in helping the other student. This is what an empowered music student looks like.

All students have something valuable to share, and they need to know how to share their ideas appropriately, work well with others, identify how they learn best, and advocate for themselves. We can teach them these skills. Sometimes we work with them on finding a better way to communicate with others or help them see they have something valuable to offer a group. Still other times it's helping a student figure out what they need (a break, a fidget toy, a quiet space, a wobble stool, or a visual planner) to be successful in the situation. By empowering them, we can be the "guide on the side" and step in only when they need our help.

Kathryn: I'm reminded of the time I taught a sword dance to a group of fourth graders. Near the end of the dance, students put their swords (meter sticks) together to form a star. One group was having a hard time putting their star together. I could see their error and stopped to help them. They were engaged in the activity and didn't want my help. I was frustrated because I could have solved the problem in thirty seconds. But they weren't ready for my help. They weren't arguing with each other. They weren't frustrated with each other or the task. So I backed away, waited, and watched. If they figured it out themselves, it would be a much more powerful learning experience. If they needed my help or started to get frustrated, I would know to step in. After a few minutes, one member from the group called me over and asked for help. I had their attention, showed them the solution, and let them get back to working on the dance as a group. I learned that I have to watch and listen to what each group needs. I need to let them experience the learning and step in at just the right moment.

This has also added life back into the learning. As mentioned earlier, too many students were walking into our classrooms already disengaged with school. While many would comply, they were doing the minimum. School was being done *to* them. We wanted more for them and knew we could adjust our lessons to use a more personalized approach. We found that little shifts to what had already been planned made a large impact on our students. We started to see a light come back into their eyes as they became immersed in the learning. They also didn't wait for our permission to continue the music-making. They created outside the classroom, brought creations in from home to share, and pushed their thinking forward all on their own. The process doesn't happen overnight, but slow shifts can shape instruction to create a much richer and meaningful learning experience.

If nothing else, consider making the shift toward student empowerment because it's fun for both your students and you! They'll enjoy class even more, and you will enjoy teaching it. Planning for classes and knowing the opportunities students will have can't be beat! This doesn't come without some hard work and preparation. There are days when it will be tough and you may want to just return to the old tried-and-true lesson plans and days when it feels like it would be easier to just tell the students what they need to know. But try to take joy in not knowing where the class period may go—not knowing what your students may latch on to and run with. And then take joy in the happiness they display when they make the music really come to life. It's worth the effort!

Are You Ready?

Sometimes we get pushback from teachers who assume that our classrooms are full of students listening only to their favorite music or the latest YouTube sensation. Please know that is not the case. As music teachers, we have the responsibility of working through the curriculum, teaching students proper techniques and fundamentals necessary for performance, while exposing them to high-quality repertoire in a variety of musical genres. Still, we know there is more to it. By understanding intrinsic motivation and changing our instruction slightly, we allow our students to navigate the content so they can own it. Kindergarten students can do this, as well as high schoolers. Students will busy themselves with work the day before winter break. They'll come back from summer vacation and ask about a project completed the year before.

The work is legitimate, real, and necessary. We can guide our students into becoming fine young musicians who are self-starters, who persevere when the learning gets difficult. In a world that changes so quickly, they will need to adapt, create, reflect, and collaborate—all without the aid of a teacher. Those skills don't happen overnight. It takes modeling, repetition, and plenty of opportunities to empower learners. If we want more from our students, we need to change their learning experiences in the music classroom. It starts with each and every one of us. Are you ready to empower your students? Are you ready to pass the baton?

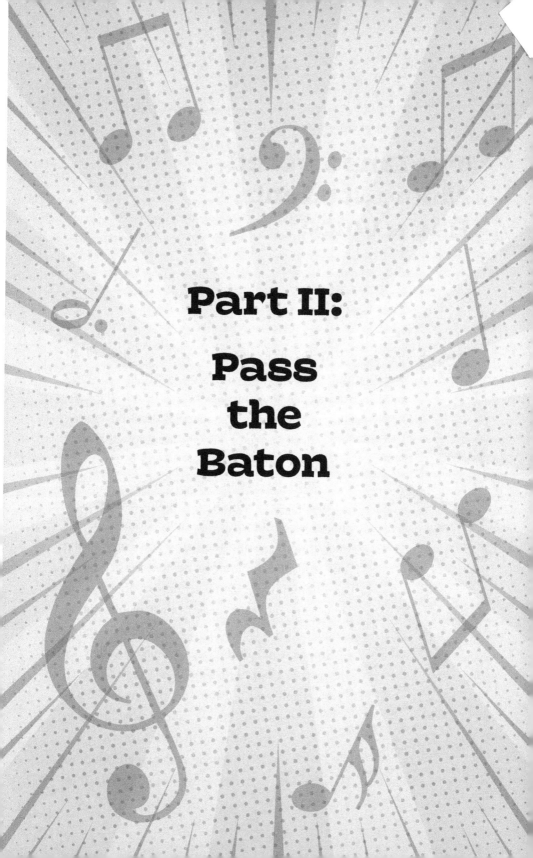

Part II:

Pass the Baton

4

The Empowered
Music Student
Has a Voice

Each chapter in Part II will explain one of the qualities of an empowered music student and offer basic examples of ways we've incorporated it into our classrooms. While the concepts might address a specific situation—vocal, general, or instrumental—please know that they are interchangeable. It's up to you to find their specific relevance in your own classroom. We'll also suggest "Things to Try Tomorrow," describing small shifts you can employ immediately to work toward passing the baton and empowering your students. We understand that for a book to be meaningful, it must be actionable. To only read something and gain ideas from it would not be enough. The "Things to Try Tomorrow" section will give you specific ways to make a difference in your classroom. Finally, at the end of each chapter, we'll feature another music educator as an "Encore," showcasing how they are changing their classrooms.

When students are empowered, they're in control of their

learning process. Initially, this can sound like an overwhelming idea. To make it easier, we've defined six qualities that all students should experience. By ensuring that your own students do so throughout the year, you'll be on the road to empowering them. The empowered music student:

- ♪ has a voice
- ♪ has a choice
- ♪ creates and consumes
- ♪ asks questions
- ♪ is connected
- ♪ owns the learning process

Student voice may sound redundant for a music classroom, but we assure you, it is not. When students have a voice, their thoughts are heard and valued. They feel safe to share their opinions, questions, and ideas.

According to Laurie Barron and Patti Kinney, authors of *Middle School: A Place to Belong and Become*, research has proven that honoring student voice improves learning. Students whose voices are heard are more motivated and involved in the learning process. They're more committed to being valued members of the class.[1] We've found all of these to be true in our own classrooms! When they have a voice in choosing repertoire, a voice in their next steps in their small lesson group, or a chance to share their reflections about a recent performance, they are eager to come to class, perform their best, and extend their musicianship outside of the school day.

Start by making sure your students know that what they have to say is important. What are they interested in? What do they love about music? What don't they love? They should know that, above

Start by making sure your students know that what they have to say is important.

all, you care about them. Make it a priority to know everyone's name. Use their names when talking to them. Ask them about their day and notice a new haircut.

It's also important for them to know their voices are being heard. Technology can help with this. There are many apps and tools available that allow students to share their voices through either video, audio, or text—Google tools, Flipgrid, and Seesaw are great examples. (More information about technology will be covered in Chapter 11.) Then look at what you're doing with their responses. Do you acknowledge their thoughts and opinions? Do you use their suggestions and feedback? Giving them a voice encourages them to think critically, offer feedback, and reflect on their work.

Musical Voice

Find ways for individuals or small groups to perform for you, in front of the class, or even for a small outside audience. Consider allowing students to play a piece they are working on at home. Some teachers offer a share day, while others have students share whenever they ask and are ready. Often when students are preparing for an audition, we'll encourage them to play some of the audition piece for the class. Not only does this give them the chance to practice for the audition, but it's also an easy way for them to share their musical voices.

The simple act of asking for student volunteers to demonstrate a passage or musical skill you are working on in class does a lot pedagogically, and also empowers those students. You recognize that they have valuable musical contributions to make, and their fellow students will respond well to peer models. It can take very little time for an entire section of an ensemble, or even a full class, to individually sing or play a short musical phrase. It's important when recognizing student voices, however, that we do it in a nonthreatening way. As the educator, you must do the work first to develop a safe environment. Do not use this sort of demonstration for a grade, and don't penalize students for missing a note. Recognize that students are simply sharing. If it helps, you can think of these times as formative assessments to help plan future instruction.

As John Feierabend, music education researcher and pedagogue, says, when a student shares his or her musical voice, any response is the correct response. Students are vulnerable when they share, so we should accept their responses and praise them.

Students as Leaders

Most of us have at least a couple students who take private music lessons. Give those students a chance to explain a concept to the class and become the teacher. Even the youngest of them enjoy doing this! They feel a sense of pride when they get to explain something to their peers, and their classmates tend to pay closer attention in these situations. Listening to a student teach or review a concept with his or her peers helps you determine how well that student understands.

Theresa: In my band and orchestra classes, after our warm-up routines become comfortable, I ask my students to take over leading. Sometimes, I'll tell them what skills to work on, such as a specific scale or technique. Other times, I'll ask them to choose something from a page in our lesson book. Occasionally, I give them complete freedom in choosing what to work on with the class. During this time, I'll usually take my instrument and sit in the ensemble, playing along. Some days I use it as an opportunity for formative assessment and will walk around the room observing and helping individuals. I should note: do not reserve these leadership opportunities only for the high-performing students! All students can benefit from being a leader, as long as the task is appropriate for their abilities. Teaching something furthers their own understanding.

Kathryn: Kindergarten students can be leaders too! In my class, I begin by singing a short greeting to each student. After a few months, they're all ready to be the leader and sing the greeting. I always ask for volunteers and praise each child for being the leader. They love this opportunity, and I believe we all learn so much in this short exercise. Part of our job is to help them see that they all have something important to offer. Some students in my classroom cannot speak due to physical or mental disabilities. If a student can't speak, he shakes an instrument. If a student can't speak or hold an instrument, she uses an iPad to activate a singing voice using the SoundingBoard app. There is so much power when we take the time to hear and celebrate each voice and also give that voice a chance to lead.

Group Critique

How often during a class do you stop the ensemble and tell the group what went wrong and how to fix it? Or upon stopping, how often do you tell them what they did well—everyone loves praise! Consider also asking them for their thoughts. What did they hear? What did they notice? What parts didn't feel right to them and should be isolated for further practice? What do they think went well and should be replicated each time? They might want to offer suggestions, such as inserting dynamic or tempo changes, for additional impact in the music. Next time you stop the group, ask them to complete one of the following sentences:

    ♪ I heard . . .

    ♪ I noticed . . .

    ♪ What if we tried . . .

Students must listen to what is happening in their section and the ensemble as they play, think about what they have just played, and in general think critically about the music itself.

Sharing Class Activities

Students love to share their learning. In the elementary school setting, they love sharing with another class. Often classrooms pair up and read together, play together on a field day, or collaborate on a fun holiday activity. Sometimes Kathryn will have fifth graders invite a fourth-grade class to hear a ukulele performance. Then, after the fifth graders perform, she'll break the class into small groups and ask the fifth graders to share beginner basics for the ukulele with the fourth graders. Performing for a buddy class is a safe way to share in school.

Sharing our learning with others gives learning a purpose and sends a message that what we are doing is important. More and more teachers join social media each day, not only to connect personally with friends and family but also to share with other teachers, classrooms, and parents. When teachers get their classes on social media, parents gain a view into the classroom, see friendly reminders of upcoming events, and connect what their children learn in class to what they do at home.

Another suggestion takes this one step further. What if your students had a say in what was shared? We're not asking you to hand over control of a Facebook page to a fifth grader, but what if each class period there was one student responsible for documenting and drafting a social media post, showcasing what they learned that day? Or they could request to have a particular song or activity shared on the class social media page. Music is meant to be shared, and giving our students the opportunity to showcase their learning with a global audience is a powerful thing! Below are some ideas to think about as you encourage student voices online.

We have separate social media accounts for our classrooms. Here we post pictures and videos (only if families have completed the school's media release form), promote events, and share other musical anecdotes. The intended audience is parents, other teachers or classes in our county, and other music teachers around the world.

In Theresa's classroom, students can also apply to be "social media interns." She encourages them to create a social media post that captures their learning for the day. Using their school iPads, they submit tweets—pictures, video, and text—to her via Google Forms, and then she takes care of posting. The students love it! One was especially excited when her tweet about a piece they were learning caught the attention of the composer!

Announce concert details on social media as a
helpful reminder to parents.

A band composer responds to a social media intern's tweet.

Some years Theresa adds another role, class historian. The historian has a similar job description, to record one great thing that happened in class that day. The historian writes their contribution on a Post-it Note and places it with those from previous days and from other classes on a poster in the back of the classroom. Everyone can view this poster and see what's been posted. Theresa has also used this with younger students as a way of training them to become social media interns the following year. Students are proud of what they do, and they should share their successes with the world—and their failures as well, to show the challenges they face. This can also be a great opportunity for them to see what other classes are doing.

Historians share the great things happening in music class.

In high schools or middle schools, there's a good chance that students will follow the class social media page. We should encourage this! For elementary school students, it's much less likely, because parents are more apt to be concerned about exposing them to social media. We discovered a way for them to safely view their posts without having to actually *be* on social media. Using a tool called Wakelet, we can curate all the social media intern tweets and others we post. The students follow a link to a Wake (collection) and can view the tweets without ever going near Twitter. It works great. They enjoy seeing what their classmates post and the replies they receive. If your department or school has a TV on display, consider submitting a social media slideshow for all to see.

The level at which your students can share their voices on social media will depend on your school's policy and the age of your students. Some teachers in districts with very strict social media policies have enabled students to share their voices in a music class newsletter, distributed to parents via email. High school teachers may find the opposite to be the case in terms of policy and can give student leaders control of the ensemble Facebook page or Instagram account. Every situation is different. It may take some trial and error to determine what works for you, and it will probably require training for the students involved. We will discuss social media more in Chapter 8.

If you're looking for a resource to learn more about giving students a voice in this way, check out the book *Social LEADia*, written by Jennifer Casa-Todd.[2] When you see the amazing things students are doing, it will inspire you to take a risk and push the envelope.

Concert Announcements and Program Notes

Many of us have narrated during a concert or musical program to fill time between pieces and educate the audience about the performance. We've researched and compiled notes about a particular composer or piece of music. Sometimes we've even used this research to create scripts for students to read, giving them another way to be involved during concerts. Why not have them own this part of the process too? Allow them to write the song introductions and read them. For younger students, you may provide the publisher's written description to work with, while older students should be able to do the research themselves. It's much more meaningful when they can contribute their own thoughts about a piece of music. You're giving them a chance for their voices to be heard and therefore an opportunity to have more ownership over the process.

If you want to give more students the opportunity to have their voices heard in this way, consider having *all* of them write introductions to performance pieces, either as individuals or in small groups. Compile the introductions on a Padlet, in a Google Doc, or using a similar digital platform, and share this with parents at the performance. Then select several students to read their introductions at the concert. By doing this, you give everyone a voice in the process. When preparing for some concerts, we've divided the ensemble into groups and assigned each group a piece to write about. The students would then elect one or two members from their group to read the introduction at the concert. A colleague did something similar and asked students to answer three questions in their introduction:

1. Why do you think we sang this piece in chorus?
2. What has this piece taught you about singing?
3. What is something interesting about the piece or one detail the audience should listen for?

Just as with any activity, adjust it to meet the needs of your learners. The more comfortable your students become, the more freedom you can give them. As an interesting side note, at one school we frequently received administrator feedback about whether or not the students were clear when speaking into the microphone at concerts. We've noticed that when students write their introductions, this feedback is much more positive! They speak confidently and clearly, as they feel the importance of the words they wrote.

Ask for Student Feedback

Throughout the school year, ask your students for their feedback. What do they like about music class? What would they like to see changed? Ask them open-ended questions both about the content and your teaching. You can even ask about the classroom environment. Kathryn asked her students what they needed in the classroom, and they came up with great ideas, like a recording studio, a green screen, and a variety of seating options. There were some suggestions she didn't take them up on (such as a classroom pet and a couch). She controlled the classroom makeover, in other words, but the students appreciated the changes she made due to their suggestions.

When asking your students for feedback on a project or performance, push them to think beyond good or bad. Ask them to think critically about why they feel a certain way. We want them to think critically about everything, such as their musical preferences, their performances, and the performances of others. We want them to clearly articulate their thoughts about these topics. With younger students, or those new to thinking this way, begin by asking questions or providing sentence starters, having them complete a phrase:

♪ One thing I like about music class is _____
♪ One thing I hope we do in music class is _____
♪ One piece of advice I would give next year's class is _____
♪ Participating in _____ taught me _____
♪ One thing I wish my music teacher knew is _____
♪ If I could change something about _____ it would be _____
♪ My favorite part of _____ was _____

These activities don't have to take an entire class period. It can be a quick bell ringer or exit ticket, where students write one- or two-sentence responses at the beginning or end of class. You might have them reflect on their performance of a piece in rehearsal, then have them place a tally mark on the board stating whether they feel the piece is uncomfortable, comfortable, or mastered. Be sure to reference their feedback the next class period and use that information to guide rehearsal. It's amazing how quickly students will respond to you when they realize you took the time to read their comments and valued what they were thinking. You may not get to do this activity often, but when you do, the effect is powerful.

Another way to encourage student voice is to ask for feedback before you start a big project. Kathryn's fifth-grade students generated some great ideas before learning how to play the ukulele. She asked them to create a video in Seesaw to share what they hoped to learn and do with the instrument. Because of the feedback they learned a variety of songs they were interested in playing, and they used the ukuleles in their spring musical. They saw their ideas turn into action. Asking students for their feedback proves you value their voices. But never acknowledging their responses may be more damaging than not asking at all. Understand that not all feedback will be equally valuable to you, but each comment is valuable to the student who provided it.

Taking Student Voice a Step Further

"Voice and choice" is a common phrase heard when educators are talking about personalized learning—however, giving students a voice means more than hearing what a child has to say. Bena Kallick and Allison Zmuda define "student voice" as "involvement and engagement in 'the what' and 'the how' of learning early in the learning process." While this is a much more complex vision of student voice, it's also a way for you to truly empower students, as in this situation they have a say in what they learn and how they learn it.

The first step of this process is a *teacher-centered* approach. The teacher and students work together to set goals based on the students' strengths, challenges, and interests. In the music classroom, this might look like the teacher sharing his or her goals for an upcoming project, unit, or performance and each student identifying their comfort level and setting one personal goal. For example, in a guitar class, after they've learned basic technique, the teacher might tell students they will learn four new chords over the next several class periods. The teacher's goal could be for them to use those chords with the proper hand position and technique while playing songs. The students would then identify their current comfort level with guitar technique and set a goal for how many or which specific songs they will learn.

Once everyone is comfortable with this level of student voice, the next step is for the students to take a more active role, which is *learner-centered*. Students identify the steps needed to achieve a goal and contribute to designing lessons, projects, assessments, and performances. The teacher can provide a variety of resources for students to use, or students may look outside the classroom to find their own. Advanced students may decide to learn skills beyond the class expectations, such as new playing techniques. They may determine when they're ready to learn new chords on the guitar, decide what their next set of skills will be, and choose a personal goal to show they have achieved mastery.

Finally, student voice becomes *learner-driven*. Students identify the problems or objectives and generate solutions, driving the learning experience.[3] Achieving this level of voice and metacognition—the ability to analyze one's thinking—is necessary for the most thorough reflection and goal setting. Students will continually reflect on their guitar playing, setting goals for themselves and determining the necessary steps for attainment. This could include finding a variety of resources to learn from, using online and print materials, creating performance opportunities such as open mic nights, and collaborating with other musicians inside or outside of the class. The teacher is still there as a mentor and guide, but the student has taken ownership of the process.

The tendency is to set goals then reflect, when in reality it should be the other way around. To effectively set a goal, students should take into consideration where they are now, where they hope to be, and what it will take for them to get there. This will help determine if the goal is achievable. This is true of your goals for the class also. If your goal for the band is to perform Holst's First Suite in E-flat (grade 5) in the spring, but currently they can only perform music at a grade 1, the goal is likely not achievable. But if you first reflect on where the students are musically, choosing a piece that is a grade 1.5 or 2 is more reasonable. First Suite can be a long-term goal, but there needs to be something more achievable in the short term. Similarly, if a student's goal is to perform a complex aria in French, but he or she has never sung in a foreign language, a better goal might be to learn a basic French aria and work up to the more complex one.

Reflecting

There are many ways students can reflect on their work. A simple self-assessment after a playing assignment or a performance task is a great place to start. Ask them to evaluate themselves on a scale of 1 to 4:

1–I don't understand this skill at all.

2–I understand the skill, but need more practice.

3–I understand this skill and can apply it.

4–I am an expert at this skill and could teach it to others.

A self-assessment of this type doesn't have to take much time. Students could put their name and selected numbers on a Post-it Note and stick it on the door as they are leaving the classroom, or they could draw a check mark in the appropriate category on the board. The point is to have students reflect on their current level of achievement.

For deeper reflection, have students provide more details. This can be done by writing responses, on paper or digitally, or by having them record videos of their responses. You may choose to provide students with prompts, such as:

♪ I was good at _____

♪ I liked _____

♪ I had problems with _____

♪ I would like to get better at _____

♪ Next time, I might _____

You could ask your students to write letters to themselves, explaining the learning process they are going through and the steps they've taken. This is especially valuable when they're working on independent tasks, such as preparing for a solo or a small ensemble performance. Encouraging them to reflect on their current practice habits and routines will also be worthwhile.

Remember that reflection should not only occur at the end of something—after a concert or at the end of the semester or year. Ideally it should take place throughout the process so students can do something with their reflections. Their reflections will be most useful if they can use it to grow as musicians. Remind them to be specific in their reflections. As a teacher, don't be afraid to ask why in response to a student's observation about his or her performance. They might be tempted to write something like, "My performance was good." By asking them why, you force them to give a concrete example. Continue asking why until you get to the heart of the matter. The more students practice self-reflection, the more powerful the exercise will become.

Goal Setting

Once your students are comfortable reflecting on their progress and performance, they are ready to set goals for themselves. As with other things mentioned in this book, start small and build upon this process, especially if students have never set their own goals before. Many will set goals that are too vague ("my goal is to play better") or that are unreasonable ("my goal is to play everything perfectly") if they have not already learned goal-setting techniques.

Model goal setting for students. Review a class goal you all recently worked on, establishing what a good goal looks like. Anything that will get students in the mindset of setting specific, measurable goals will work. Even if it's still teacher-centered, you're helping them learn a skill. Next, have them work with a partner or small group to create a goal. Maybe the goal is to perform a scale at a specific tempo three times in a row. Eventually, they should be able to reflect on their current state and set relevant, meaningful goals. It's when they set their own goals that the why behind what you do in the classroom becomes more apparent to them and they can begin to take more ownership.

It may be helpful to have your students work within the SMART goal framework. Various iterations and interpretations of SMART goals have surfaced, but the basic understanding is that SMART goals contain the following elements:

S–specific

M–measurable

A–achievable

R–relevant

T–time bound

You can use SMART goals in many settings; they're currently part of the teacher evaluation process in several states. Teaching students to set SMART goals will not only help them activate their voices in music class, it will give them access to yet another life skill.

Other things that will make goal setting more meaningful:

♪ Write the goal somewhere it can be easily accessed.

♪ Understand what steps will be necessary to achieve the goal—write these as well.

♪ Monitor the goal and refer back to it frequently.

♪ Have others invested in the process—other teachers and parents—or have your students find an "accountability buddy."

♪ Know that it's okay to adjust or revise a goal.

♪ Celebrate success, not necessarily with prizes, but share the great news.

Goal setting has gone through many iterations in our classes. In instrumental music, the students work through a list of competencies, basic skills we want them to learn as band or orchestra students. They work at their own pace and have a lot of freedom and choice. At the beginning of each quarter, they evaluate how they feel about specific skills: Is the skill mastered, familiar, or unfamiliar? This is the initial reflection. Then they set a goal for how many new skills they will demonstrate mastery of that quarter.

The first time we do this is an eye-opening experience for everyone! Many students want to set goals that are much too difficult for their current playing level or practicing habits. Others set goals so low they aren't learning anything new. But we work together throughout the process to find goals that are a comfortable stretch—both achievable and relevant.

Dedicating class time to reflecting and goal setting can be challenging. We have limited time with our students each week, and the impulse is to spend as much of it as possible making music! Trust that spending a few minutes reflecting and goal setting will be worth it. It's similar to the time spent on fundamentals. Sometimes we want to rush through them to get to the "real" music-making, the literature. In reality, the time spent on fundamentals will strengthen the ability to perform the literature. Taking the time to reflect and set goals enables more purposeful music-making for each student.

Having one-on-one conferences is ideal, but not always possible with large classes and limited time. Don't be afraid to get creative! Technology can assist you, allowing you to respond to students at another time, either by video or text. One trick when providing typed responses to students is to dictate the comments. Most people can speak more clearly and accurately than they type, which will save time. For older students, you may find that a reflection and goal-setting journal, either paper or digital, could be useful.

> **Taking the time to reflect and set goals enables more purposeful music-making for each student.**

Coda

Anytime you give students a voice in your classroom, whether it's through assigning them a leadership role, having them act as a social media intern, or getting them to introduce songs for a concert, you can give those who may not be the best musicians a place to shine. Some struggle in the music classroom. They enjoy playing an instrument, but it doesn't come as easily for them. These students still love the opportunity to share on social media the successes from a rehearsal, to speak at concerts, and to perform many other duties. It helps them feel like valued, contributing members of the group. We know our impact as teachers can often go much deeper than just music.

Make opportunities, regardless of how small, for students to give feedback on their musical experiences, reflect on their personal progress and achievements, and set goals for themselves as musicians and as learners. When you take student voice a step further in a way that directly impacts the classroom and their music-making, you are truly passing the baton!

Things to Try Tomorrow

♪ Ask a volunteer to demonstrate a musical passage during class.

♪ Invite students to perform for the class something they are working on independently.

♪ If your class is on social media, challenge students to come up with one thing they learned that day to share on the class page. This could even be an exit-ticket activity at the end of class.

♪ When stopping a piece during rehearsal, ask your students to share what they heard before you give your own thoughts.

♪ Find something that is routine—that you do regularly during class—and ask for a student volunteer to lead this activity instead.

♪ Before a performance, ask the students how they would introduce each piece. How would they describe it to an audience? What were their favorite parts of preparing the piece?

♪ Ask students to reflect on a recent activity or performance and list one "glow" and one "grow" (something that went well and something that may still require more work).

♪ Share with your students one of your goals for the next unit or performance. As a class, work together to set another goal.

Continue the conversation:
share what you tried with
#PasstheBatonBook!

Encore: Personalized Concert Welcomes with Keith Ozsvath

Keith Ozsvath, director of instrumental music at Rotolo Middle School in Batavia, Illinois, found a unique way for his students to share their voices: he had them create individual videos to welcome friends and family to their winter concert! A few weeks before the concert, the students reflected on the pieces they were performing and identified something in the music that excited them. Using a template, they created scripts and recorded their videos in Flipgrid, a video response tool.

Students used rehearsal time to write their scripts, enabling them to be both thoughtful and reflective. Keith created a recording schedule so they knew exactly when they would make their own videos. The schedule allowed sufficient time for them all to record and provided extra time for those who needed to rerecord or missed their scheduled slot.

After all of Keith's students completed their videos, he downloaded a QR code for each. The QR codes were saved in a folder, naming each file with the student's name. He then created a document template to display each name, QR code, and the school logo on a separate page. Each page was printed and displayed in the hallway for families to view before the concert.

Keith reported that the uniqueness of the project created excitement in the band room. Students found this project highly engaging and were very eager to record their welcome videos. Many added creative touches, such as a personalized message to their family members or a short melody played on their instrument, in addition to the script template that Keith had provided. Not only were they engaged, but the project gave them an opportunity to reflect on their own learning as musicians.

Keith added, "I believe there was an extra incentive for the students to perform their music at a high level because of the reflective welcome videos." His advice to others is: "Just do it! The students will love creating a video and crafting a personalized message to their parents and other family members attending the concert. The 'key' to having a successful project is planning everything out, with enough time to allow for mistakes. If the class is new to Flipgrid, teach the students how to use it first. Then work on the steps of the project for implementation."

Connect with Keith!

- ♪ Blog—teachingmusicandmore.com
- ♪ Email—kaozsvath@gmail.com
- ♪ Facebook—facebook.com/TeachingMusicandMore/
- ♪ Twitter—@keithozsvath

5

The Empowered Music Student Has a Choice

Empowered music students must be given choices. This is something we can all relate to; everyone appreciates having choices! Think about professional development (PD) training. Which would be more beneficial: having every teacher in the district attend the same training, or giving them a choice based on interest, prior knowledge, and subject area? Most of us would choose the second option. We don't want to sit through training on something that is much too easy or difficult for us, and we don't want to attend a workshop that isn't relevant to our subject area. Even if we're only given two options, most of us still appreciate the choice. As educators, we seek powerful PD that we find purpose in, that gives us a choice in the new learning, and that we find challenging so that it pushes our thinking forward.

Students don't differ much from adults in this sense. They appreciate being given choices, especially when we take their interests, abilities, and strengths into account. Powerful learning begins when we can tap into their intrinsic motivation. We again reference Daniel Pink, the author of *Drive*, and his belief that all humans need autonomy, mastery, and purpose to be motivated. When students feel autonomy, the ability to act upon their own choices, they are on the path to becoming intrinsically motivated. Pink found the following benefits to autonomous motivation: "greater conceptual understanding, better grades, enhanced persistence at school and in sporting activities, higher productivity, less burnout, and greater levels of psychological well-being."[1] When students have choices, they'll have a better understanding of the musical content they're working with, be more persistent when working on difficult skills and techniques, and enjoy their music-making more!

Mike Anderson, the author of *Learning to Choose, Choosing to Learn: The Key to Student Motivation and Achievement*, believes there are two main reasons to give students choice in the classroom. First, because it teaches them to self-differentiate; they can choose work that is appropriately challenging. Second, choice enables them to tap into their own interests and passions, becoming more invested in their learning. This is exactly what we want for our empowered music students!

Our first responsibility as music teachers is to create an environment where students feel safe and supported in their learning. Next, we must offer good choices, keeping in mind the various interests, strengths, and needs of the students. When we help them understand how to identify good choices for themselves, we increase the likelihood of success. Encourage them to think about which option they would enjoy the most, which would provide an appropriate challenge, and which would best help them learn. The more choices they make, the more they'll become comfortable with the process.[2]

Allowing your students to make choices is possibly one of the most important ways you can empower them in the music classroom. By giving them choices, you're automatically honoring and encouraging their voices. Sometimes, just by reflecting on your own instruction, you will see how you can offer more choice in a lesson. Start with lessons you've already planned. Is there something little you could shift that would offer a bit more choice for your students?

Musical Choices

Many students become reliant on the teacher to make all musical choices for them. They're taught, for example, that the teacher knows the "right" way to perform a piece and that's how it must always be done. However, as professionals, we know there are exceptions to all rules! Different interpretations of a single piece of music exist, and that's okay. By having choices in the music-making process, students feel more connected to what they perform, and as a result they feel more ownership of the learning. You're also teaching them how to make musical decisions, which is something all independent musicians should know. We want them to start at a young age so they won't be afraid of these decisions later in life.

As always, start small. You might ask your students to choose what dynamic level a piece should be performed at, or to pick motions to do during a movement activity. Consider having them try a piece two ways, once slowly and again fast, and then ask them to choose which way to perform it. As they're deciding, ask them to defend their decisions. Ask something like "why does it sound better performed at a faster tempo?" or "what in the music makes you think that is the most appropriate choice?" Now they're not only getting to decide, but they are selecting, analyzing, and reflecting on their own musical choices. When working on pieces that are considered "standard repertoire," share with them why you've made certain choices about the piece or why you believe others made their choices. This lays the groundwork for them to transfer and apply these techniques to other pieces later in the year.

Kathryn: In my elementary school music room, students learn to play classroom instruments with the proper technique by performing sound effects during a story. Often, the specific words and instruments are predetermined. But do they need to be?

Now I've made the shift to read the sound story to them and let *them* decide how and when instrument sounds would be appropriate. Students love to choose the instruments, and they are often highly engaged when they collaborate on the final creation. With this little shift, they're trying different instruments, reflecting on their choices, and making adjustments as they create.

Choice in Seating

Do you have an assigned seat at faculty meetings? What about during professional development? Many of us have probably attended professional events where we've been told where to sit. How can someone else know where it will be best for us to sit? Now think about how your students must feel, being told class after class where to sit in the room and in relationship to their peers. Some educators talk about the "Starbucks model" when discussing classroom seating, referring to the multiple options a customer has for enjoying his or her beverage at Starbucks. There are comfy armchairs, long tables, bar-top tables, and even chairs outside. Each space serves a different purpose, and that's why people like having the choice. Consider the same thing for your classroom. Do you have different seating options available for different purposes?

Giving your students the opportunity to choose their seats is an easy way to put them in control of their learning. So many of us spend hours lamenting over seating charts. There can be value in this—accommodating student needs, helping to learn names, balancing instrumentation, and just plain having control! But ask yourself: Do students always *have* to sit in these assigned seats? Give them a choice. If there is no distinct pedagogical reason for your seating chart, consider allowing them to make that seating choice for themselves occasionally.

There are many hidden benefits to having students choose their own seats. In performance ensembles, allowing them to sit where they want indirectly forces them to focus more on their music. When they sit in the same assigned seat over and over, they come to rely on those sitting on either side of them. They also get different perspectives now.

A tuba player only ever sees and hears the conductor from a distance, so he or she will have a very different experience sitting in the front row. Some teachers will put stools in the percussion section, allowing wind players to experience the music-making from that perspective. In our ensembles, we aim to give students this choice in seating at least once each concert cycle. Sometimes we'll stay in the mixed seating just for warm-ups, other times for the entire rehearsal. Our students are quick to remind us if we haven't used a mixed seating in a while, as they enjoy having this choice and change of pace.

They could also have a choice in where to sit in a general music classroom. They might choose a seat at a table, a place on the carpet, or any other seating in your classroom. Encourage your students to sit somewhere that will enable them to make good choices and be their best musical selves throughout the class period. When working in groups or individually, students appreciate finding their own workspace in the music room. Depending on the age of the student, some will have difficulty making a good choice. When this arises—and it will—you are there to guide them.

Even if you can only occasionally have students choose where they sit, doing so at any time silently tells them that you trust them. You trust them to make a good decision. You trust them to do what is best for themselves and the group. That trust is so vitally important if you want them to open themselves up to being vulnerable and making music. Building that trust, and building that relationship, is worth any inconvenience it may cause you.

Skill Mastery

Another opportunity to offer choice is when your students are learning specific musical skills. Instead of focusing on individual songs you'd like the students to learn, figure out the underlying skill that's important and make that the requirement. There are likely a variety of songs they could learn to show they've mastered that skill, so why not give them a choice? This gives them options in what to practice—and many times results in them playing more than they would have if they'd all been assigned one song. They can choose songs that interest them and are appropriately challenging. Having that choice makes them feel more in control of the learning process.

Theresa made this shift to focusing on skills when she was teaching beginning band and orchestra classes. She now gives students a list of learning targets to work toward mastering. Along with each learning target, she provides three suggested songs to play to show mastery. In addition, there's a student choice option, where they can choose any song they would like to demonstrate mastery of the skill. They appreciate the variety of options.

Most of Theresa's students pick one of the suggested songs, which is just fine. Others, who are looking for a challenge or have an interest in learning different music, use the student choice option. One student played various Christmas songs for several of his learning targets from winter through spring! This was fine too, because he was practicing music and learning new skills. At the end of the day, that's what's important.

Learning Target	Option 1	Option 2	Option 3	Option 4 Student Choice** (write song name)	✔
1. I can play songs with 3 notes.	#17 Hot Cross Buns	#6 Moving On Up	#8 Four by Four		
2. I can keep my air flowing for at least 6 counts, AND separate notes with my tongue.	#14 Rolling Along	#18 Go Tell Aunt Rhodie	#23 March Steps		
3. I can perform the new note #27.	#31 Mozart Melody	#28 Claire De La Lune	#30 London Bridge - top line		
4. I can perform with changes in dynamics.	#38 Jingle Bells	#39 My Dreydl	#45 William Tell		

Example of fourth-grade band learning targets

While we used this technique for band and orchestra, it could work in many areas! When teaching voice or piano, let your students choose some skill-related tasks they plan to practice for the following week's lesson (pick flash cards or an app for note learning, choose a specific song for skill practice, highlight trouble spots to focus on, etc.). Consider how you could give them a choice in demonstrating their mastery playing the recorder, ukulele, guitar, or any number of other instruments.

Performance Repertoire

One of our roles as music educators is to expose our students to high-quality music, both for listening and performing. Many of us spend significant time studying and researching diverse repertoire for this purpose. The next time you're programming for a concert or performance, consider giving your students a choice. Select two or three pieces that would fit your goals for the ensemble and ask them which they prefer. This can turn into a great exercise in sight-reading, listening, or score analysis, as they'll have to pay critical attention before casting their votes. Students appreciate being a part of the programming process and will often work hardest on this piece because they chose it. In fact, several times when we've given them a choice, our students have picked the more difficult option! Whatever factors contributed to the piece being the favorite outweighed the extra work it would be to perform.

If having your students choose music for a performance isn't possible, there still could be other options. For instance, they could choose music to use as sight-reading practice for an ensemble. Many older students would enjoy spending time in the music library, searching for music for this purpose. Depending on the age and depth of your library, they might find some hidden gems during this process!

They can also choose the repertoire for small informances. Informances are informational performances, sometimes held in the music room, with the purpose of sharing with others what music class looks like on a daily basis. If students are preparing an informance for a buddy class, ask them to think about their buddies and come up with a short presentation they think their friends will like. This may be a ukulele demonstration or possibly a short presentation of a children's book with song, instruments, and movement. When we do this, we brainstorm a handful of ideas as a group, and after a discussion of each one, we vote as a class and create a plan of action. After all content has been taught and practiced, we delegate assignments and together choose the setup of the classroom and make many other artistic decisions that come up along the way while putting together a small informance.

Many educators fear that if they allow students to choose their own repertoire, they'll only pick what they know. It's definitely a possibility. This is when we can ask ourselves why they chose that music. Most likely it's because the music is relevant to them and their lives. For a middle school student, it might be difficult to find relevance in a folk song. That doesn't mean we shouldn't program the folk songs; it just means that it's okay to have a balance. We can teach them why we make the choices we do and encourage them to look for similar reasons when making their own. We can set up guidelines and parameters to help them when selecting repertoire. Sometimes we don't give our students enough credit. They can make these choices, and more often than not they'll surpass our expectations!

Choice Boards and Other Creative Ideas

There are many creative ways to give students choice in class, aside from saying, "Choose between options 1, 2, and 3." Some teachers will create a choice board, which is essentially a sheet of paper or digital document containing multiple options for students to select from. To make this more interesting, consider adding one of the following elements:

Must-dos and may-dos

You provide students with specific activities they must do and additional activities they can choose to do. The must-do activities will often contain content all students must be able to understand or do, while the may-do activities will provide extension opportunities. For example, when learning about a specific composer, all students must read the provided article about his or her life, but then they can choose one or more extension activities to learn about the composer's famous works, childhood, or performance experiences.

Menu

Students are given choices within the course of a meal: the appetizer, entrée, and dessert. You might tell them to choose one item for each course, or have one required course and others that contain options. For example, if orchestra students were working on playing in the key of G major, you might tell them that their appetizer must be the G-major scale. But for their entrée, they could have a choice of standard pieces in the key of G major, maybe from a method book. And then dessert could be a choice of fun (as in kid-friendly) pieces in G major.

Tic-Tac-Toe

As with the menu, students are given a board with multiple options. But this time the board contains nine squares, like a tic-tac-toe board. The students must complete the activities in three different boxes to get tic-tac-toe. This would also work as a bingo board . . . you would just need even more activity options!

These choice options can be used in multiple settings, such as stations in a general music class, practice assignments for performance classes, or even as challenges for student assessments. The students can work at their own pace and choose options that are the most interesting and appropriate to them. The only limit is your creativity.

One word of caution: while choice boards of any type are a great step toward empowering students, they are still very teacher-centric since you are the one creating all of the choices. At the beginning you'll need to start small, offering one to three specific options. Then gradually begin giving your students more freedom. Maybe your tic-tac-toe board includes a "Student Choice" space in the middle, where they can insert their own relevant activity. Eventually, you want to be in a place where they're mostly choosing on their own—not every activity, lesson, or assessment, but when appropriate. It could be fun to allow the class to create their own choice board. With time, they know what is appropriate and meaningful, and often their ideas are more creative than ours!

Tonight's Menu: Dynamics in Music
Learning Target #4 - I can perform a song with changes in dynamics

Soup

Listen to this piece of music,
"In the Hall of the Mountain King"
What do you notice about the volume?

Appetizers: Choose 2 or more

- Dynamics = how loudly or softly a piece of music is played
- Words describing dynamics: piano, mezzo-piano, mezzo-forte, forte
- Words describing changes in dynamics: crescendo, decrescendo
- Infographic
- Videos:
  - Video #1
  - Video #2
  - Video #3
- Music Dictionary: read definitions and hear examples of each term

Entrée: Choose 1 or more

- Use Quizlet to help learn the terms
- Use Socrative to quiz yourself
- Use these strategies on your instrument:
  - Play a song you know very well at various dynamic levels
  - Look for songs with changes in dynamics and practice playing them
  - Improvise (make up) a melody and play it at various dynamic levels and with changes in dynamics.

Dessert: Choose 1 to demonstrate mastery

Submit a video demonstrating mastery of this Learning Target.
1. Choose a song that contains dynamics
2. Choose a song and add dynamics to it - be sure to also include a picture of the music, indicating where you added the dynamics.
3. Compose a song with dynamics. Include a picture of the music showing the dynamics.

Coffee: Optional

Did you know there are even more dynamic symbols that composers use? Explore some of these resources to learn more.
- Kidzsearch
- Music Dictionary
- Video
Record what you learn on this Padlet.

Dynamics Choice Menu

Choice in the Lens of UDL

Universal Design for Learning (UDL) is a framework for curriculum development that focuses on ensuring that all students have the opportunity to learn. The term "universal design" actually stems from architecture and the effort to make places more accessible to people with disabilities. A ramp going into a building will help someone with a disability but also benefit elderly people, parents with strollers, and many others. The ramp gives everyone a choice in accessing the building in a way that best suits their needs.

We can apply the same concepts to our lessons. According to Barbara Bray and Kathleen McClaskey, authors of *How to Personalize Learning*, when they use the principles of UDL, "Teachers are better informed about how to universally design their instruction in order to reduce barriers to learning, as well as optimize the levels of support and challenge to meet the needs and interests of all learners in the classroom." When we create learning experiences with UDL in mind, we provide our students with multiple ways to access content, engage with the content, and express their knowledge of the content. But what does this look like in the music classroom?

Have you ever thought about how students access new material in your class? In a music history class, they might learn about a time period in music by reading a textbook, listening to a lecture, watching a video, or listening to music. A teacher would typically choose one or maybe two of those methods to teach the new material. In a general music class, when teaching students about dynamics, you might have them listen to, move to, and perform music with dynamic changes. By doing these things, you offer multiple means of access—multiple ways for students to experience a new concept. This is beneficial because we know that not everyone learns the same way. Providing multiple means of access ensures that everyone will be able to gain from the material, regardless of their learning style. And it's not just for those with learning differences—all students can benefit!

When we are empowering learners, the goal is to provide choice in key areas. For example, our instrumental music students all have their method book and an app that accompanies it. Some are more comfortable reading lines from the book, while others prefer to read from their iPads. It makes no difference to us as teachers which they use, as long as they all see the same notation. The benefit of the app is that they can also hear a recording of the song, reduce the tempo, and change the accompaniment. The point is not to sell students on either the book or the app, but to show them different options to engage with the content. They can choose whichever method will best help them learn the music.

When you are creating choices for students, think about how you can provide options that will support different learners in your curriculum and instruction. For performance assessments, could they have the option between performing for you in person and submitting a video to express their understanding of the content? When completing a reflection task, could they either write their reflections or create a video instead? With the UDL framework, students can take ownership of their learning, and you ensure that all have equal access to the musical experience. (For more information about Universal Design for Learning, check out www.cast.org.)

Student-Created Choices

Student agency is more than merely providing options for assignments. It's about empowering learners to truly understand what they need and how they can have these needs met.
—Trevor MacKenzie and Rebecca Bathurst-Hunt, *Inquiry Mindset*

Once you feel comfortable offering more choice in a lesson, the next step is to lesson plan *with* students instead of planning *for* them. As we briefly mentioned when discussing choice boards, true student choice goes beyond giving them two options. It means giving them the freedom to truly choose what is best for them as learners.

Take the plunge. Start a project in class and share with your students that you'd like their input as you try something new. While you may have a basic plan for the project, be open to their feedback and see where things go. Ask for suggestions to plan future music classes. Ask how they can showcase their learning besides the ideas you originally prepared. Of course, we must consider materials and allotted time when creating next steps. Not all student-generated ideas will be attainable, and they understand this. Often, making little shifts in your original plan to allow for student-generated choices can have a huge impact.

When you start small, the students will learn how to make choices. They will learn that sometimes you make a choice and it doesn't work out. That's when you regroup, learn from the choice, and try something new. When given the option to make choices, students learn how to fail and how to move on after failure. That may be the most valuable lesson of all. When we create an environment where failures are just mistakes and mistakes are just feedback, we teach kids how to navigate through the learning process and create their own next steps.

Coda

As we pass the baton to students, giving them a choice in music class, we're helping them learn how to make decisions. They determine what interests them, what choices are appropriate, and how to choose something that will best help them learn. While these decisions are important for them as musicians, they're also valuable throughout life! Students should make their own musical choices, experimenting with phrasing, tempo, dynamics, articulation, and more. Through this experimentation, choosing how to perform a piece of music, they learn much more than if we make all decisions for them.

Not everything in music class can be a choice, just as not everything in life is a choice. As adults, we don't have a choice about paying taxes! There will be areas in every class where students don't have a choice, and that's okay. As the teacher, you are ultimately responsible for the curriculum, the standards, and the students' safety. Those things aside, finding places for them to make choices will inevitably benefit them in music class and beyond.

Things to Try Tomorrow

♪ Allow your students to make musical choices in class, such as picking the tempo, dynamics, or instruments to use in a piece of music.

♪ Give them the opportunity to choose their seats during class or rehearsal, even if it's only for a short period of time.

♪ Ask them to choose between two different activities or songs for a warm-up.

♪ Think about a skill they are working on. Ask them to choose between two or three ways to show you they understand it.

♪ Give them the option to either watch a video or read a book/article/passage when learning something new.

**Continue the conversation:
share what you tried with
#PasstheBatonBook!**

Encore: Musical Choices in Choir
with Derrick Fox

Dr. Derrick Fox is the director of choral activities and associate professor of music at the University of Nebraska–Omaha. He's also a former
choral teacher of junior and senior high school students and an active
guest conductor and clinician. When teaching choir, Derrick realized
that he was working harder than his students, stepping in to help when
he should have given them time to grapple with the learning goals. As
a result, they didn't know as much as he'd originally assumed. To rectify
this, he began allowing them to make more musical choices and collaborate with others so they could take ownership of their music-making.

After they learn the basic pitches and rhythms for a piece they're
working on, Derrick splits the ensemble into sections. Then each section
makes musical choices based on what they've learned in class. Derrick
prepares his ensembles with lessons on vocabulary and technique before
asking students to apply the learning. Sections decide phrasing, dynamics, and when the melodic line should be emphasized or the focus shifts.
When they're comfortable with their musical choices, he asks sections
to combine and see if they still agree on their initial decisions. While
students work together, he'll listen, observe, and use that information to
tailor his instruction for future rehearsals. He can also give more individual praise and feedback this way. He now knows his students better
and can discuss individual growth more comfortably.

In other situations, he gives students a choice in programming
by having them decide what order in which to perform their concert
pieces. They work together in groups of five or more to discuss and
debate their thoughts, and they are required to give a musical rationale
for their ideas. Derrick asks, "How do you want the audience to feel at
the end of each piece? What is our purpose in terms of their emotional
journey? How do we put the music in order to set the mood we want?"

A great benefit of this process for students is learning the valuable
life lesson of having to discuss, disagree, and come to a compromise in
small groups. Derrick finds that when he gives students these choices,

they become more independent musicians and more committed to the choir program. They also know that he cares about their personal musicianship and their personal growth.

Again, he makes sure his students are comfortable with the basics and have the foundational knowledge necessary to make sound musical choices. They know that typically if the musical line goes up, they should crescendo; if the line goes down, they should decrescendo. Derrick always spends time modeling and practicing new skills and then gradually releases the control to them.

Derrick's advice to someone looking to incorporate choice in an ensemble setting is to "start with the low-hanging fruit." It doesn't have to be grand the first time; you can start with one small thing, and that will make a difference.

Connect with Derrick!

♪ Email: dafox@unomaha.edu
♪ Twitter: @Derrickf

6

The Empowered Music Student Creates and Consumes

There's an ongoing cycle of critical consuming, inspiration, and creative work.
—John Spencer and A. J. Juliani, *Empower*

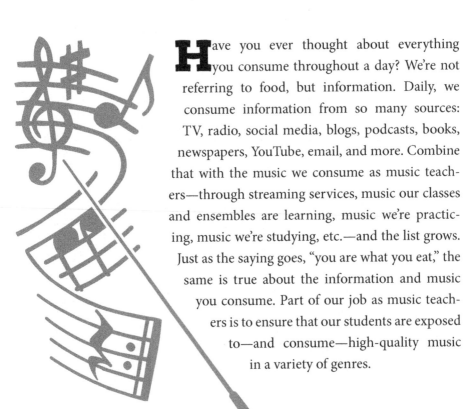

Have you ever thought about everything you consume throughout a day? We're not referring to food, but information. Daily, we consume information from so many sources: TV, radio, social media, blogs, podcasts, books, newspapers, YouTube, email, and more. Combine that with the music we consume as music teachers—through streaming services, music our classes and ensembles are learning, music we're practicing, music we're studying, etc.—and the list grows. Just as the saying goes, "you are what you eat," the same is true about the information and music you consume. Part of our job as music teachers is to ensure that our students are exposed to—and consume—high-quality music in a variety of genres.

One thing we often forget while helping our students become discerning consumers is that they must also have time to create. When we create, we use prior knowledge to make something new. Throughout the process we make revisions, reflect, and refine our learning. We can help students learn that these revisions aren't mistakes, but simply the necessary iterations that are part of the creative process. When they take risks, they gain confidence, and the understanding that risks only help them grow.

In their book *Empower,* John Spencer and A. J. Juliani define a process that takes students from being critical consumers to being creators:

1. **Awareness:** This is considered "passive exposure."
2. **Active Consuming:** You actively seek out the medium you want to consume.
3. **Critical Consuming:** You form opinions about what you are consuming and begin to become an expert.
4. **Curating:** You collect and organize your medium, often commenting on it and making connections.
5. **Copying:** After becoming an expert, you try to replicate your medium, word for word, note for note.
6. **Mash-ups:** To make something new, you combine various favorite elements that you have curated and copied.
7. **Creating from scratch:** You take big risks and make things that are original. In this stage, you have found your true voice.[1]

Most likely, many of us have experienced this process in our own musical careers. First, we explore music as it exists in our daily lives. Then we begin to seek out music of a specific genre, maybe concert band, orchestra, or choral works. Next, we form opinions on the music we listen to, making determinations about what is "good" or "desirable," making note of the characteristics we like and value. We then begin to collect or curate this music, discussing and categorizing as we go. Eventually we copy the music, trying to emulate the musicians we are listening to, possibly listening repeatedly until we get it *just right.* Then we combine aspects we were previously copying, sometimes with our own ideas, making something slightly—or even significantly—new.

Finally, we're ready to create something from scratch, whether it's an original composition or a performance of a piece done our own way. We have gone through the process, consuming to creating. Without the critical consumption, the end result may not have been possible.

Thinking about this process, we're reminded of the story wind band composer John Mackey tells about getting his start with composition. As a child, John didn't play any instruments, but he was surrounded by music and developed his interest that way. When he began writing music, he started by copying scores using a Commodore 64 computer and a music writing program called Music Construction Set. He spent hours if not days programming other people's scores (Bach, Dvořák, and Prokofiev, to name a few), which led him eventually to begin his own compositions.

Can you imagine if he had never been exposed to Bach's music, or never had the opportunity to copy Ravel's scores? Likely today there would be a noticeable gap in the wind band repertoire. Through his process of critically consuming, learning the rules, then discovering how and when to break them, Mackey was able to make his own decisions in creating his music.[2] This process is equally valuable for our students.

For them, the creation process need not be as complex as the one for John Mackey's composition projects. In fact, your students would be best served if it were not. They should start with very simple composition activities and be given these opportunities on a regular basis. All of them, regardless of age or ability level, should create often in music class. They could use instruments to create their own sound effects for a picture book, make up simple movements to a song, improvise a short melody, or compose a rhythmic ostinato. Give up a little control in the classroom and let your students do the creating.

Give up a little control in the classroom and let your students do the creating.

Improvisation

Out of the countless ways to have students create in the classroom, improvisation is a great place to start. Many definitions for improvisation and composition exist, but for this chapter we will make this distinction: Improvisation is created spontaneously and not notated. Composition does not take place spontaneously, giving the creator time to edit, revise, and thoughtfully build upon ideas. Additionally, composition is documented and can be reproduced. It can be notated, using pencil and paper, Popsicle sticks, digital notation programs, and so on, or recorded using audio or video. For these reasons, we believe starting with improvisation is a good choice for music students who are inexperienced in creating.

Regardless of the age of your students, you'll want to ease into the process of improvisation. Think back to the scaffolding we mentioned in Chapter 1. Begin by having them echo rhythmic or melodic patterns that you play. This should be something comfortable and familiar. Then, using a specific rhythm or pitch set, have them respond to what you play, as a group, with something different. A call and response. It will sound chaotic, with everyone responding differently, but it gives them the chance to try something new in a low-risk situation, because individuals cannot be heard.

Once they're comfortable with this, begin having volunteers respond to your pattern individually. Gradually increase the complexity of these exercises as it's appropriate for your students. We use improvisation activities like this frequently during the warm-up portion of rehearsals. It helps to focus the group and get creative juices flowing!

Don't assume that just because your students have been playing their instruments or singing for any number of years that they will automatically be comfortable improvising. Unless they were given these opportunities at a young age, improvisation may feel very foreign and uncomfortable to them. Make sure they know your music room is a safe space. If you've taken the time to build relationships with them early on, this will not be an issue. They must believe they can safely take risks in your classroom and trust you've prepared them with all the tools they need to succeed. Model risk-taking and celebrate any attempt. Again, as John Feierabend, music education researcher and pedagogue, says, "Any response is the right response." No matter what the student creates, say thank you!

The temptation may be to have older students improvise much more complex passages or solos. Before doing this, take into consideration their history. Is this an activity they've done before, or are they attempting it for the first time? If it's brand new, start small. You can do more damage and prolong the length of the process by forcing them into improvisation activities before they're ready. Take your time. The process is worth it.

Music Composition

Once your students have had numerous opportunities to improvise and begun learning to read music notation, they should notate music. Composition projects can look like any number of things, but depending on the age and ability of your students, scaffolding will be necessary. Just as with improvisation, make no assumptions about the students' readiness for music composition.

One common misconception is that students should have free rein when composing, but we respectfully disagree. Guidelines are not only helpful, but in most cases they are necessary. Keep in mind that you can give guidelines without setting limitations. Have your students use a specific musical element or concept in their composition. Stipulate a minimum number of beats or pitches that must be used. Students will work up to their ability level when given the option. For example, requiring them to incorporate specific pitches into their compositions but not limiting them to only those pitches will allow more advanced students to prove they understand the material while still composing at their appropriate skill level.

Mash-Ups and Arrangements

Mash-up projects are a great place to begin, especially if you are following the process John Spencer and A. J. Juliani prescribe. With a mash-up project, students start with two or more pieces of music they already know and combine them. The combining could take place in GarageBand or using a similar digital audio workstation (DAW). Students could also notate the mash-up on paper or use a digital music notation tool such as Noteflight. The purpose of the mash-up is for them to practice creating with something they already know works. We've seen students create GarageBand mash-ups of their favorite popular songs, like "Over the Rainbow" and "Fight Song," while another student wrote "Jolly Bells," a combination of "Jolly Old St. Nicholas" and "Jingle Bells" to play on his saxophone. A mash-up is a vital step in the process of moving from critically consuming to creating. Students build their musical vocabulary through mash-ups and learn rules along the way.

One benefit to having them notate their mash-up is the written manuscript practice. As they copy the score, they're automatically following music notation rules. They can also create their own arrangements of existing songs. Encourage them to create new instrumentation, harmony, form, and accompaniment. By allowing them to pick their own song to arrange, you also incorporate choice into the activity.

Jeremy Marino, a high school orchestra teacher from a northern suburb of Chicago, has his students participate in a passion project each year. They must choose a musical topic that meets three criteria: (1) it must be a topic they're interested in, (2) it must have a meaningful connection to music, and (3) the project must dive into a subject and provide them with a depth of knowledge.

Many students choose a piece and arrange it for strings using Noteflight. Jeremy allows time for all arrangements to be played by the orchestra or a small chamber group, and some pieces get featured in an orchestra program. He shared that when students see and hear their classmates' success with arranging, many experience a "lightbulb" moment, realizing that they too can create in this way. It is these kinds of moments we want our students to have and carry with them when they leave the classroom.

Original Compositions

When assigning an original composition, the first step is determining the musical goal you have for students. Original compositions can be anything from having students notate a four-beat rhythm to an entire ABA melody, or anything in between. When they create something new, without directly copying from another source, we can consider the result an original composition. Often you can use music composition to reinforce a concept or technique being taught in class. For example, if your students are learning about quarter notes and eighth notes, have them compose using these rhythms. The same could be said for teaching pitch, scales, dynamics, and more. Even better, if you can find a purpose for students' original compositions, such as intro music for a video or for the morning announcements, you will tap into their intrinsic motivation and let them create with enthusiasm!

Kathryn: Each spring, my fourth graders create a rhythmic composition. One year, I connected my classroom to Theresa's classroom to add purpose and value to this project. I brainstormed briefly with her about creating a method book. My students from Illinois could write rhythmic compositions for her students from Northern Virginia and create a fun activity to go along with each rhythmic exercise. Since peers from across the country would be using their rhythmic compositions, this would give my students a greater purpose in their rhythmic composition and a larger audience.

Theresa recorded a video message to my students in Flipgrid using a script I wrote, asking for their help in creating something fun and engaging to use at the end of the school year. My students watched the video and as a group brainstormed what they might create for the method book. Some classes ran with it and were excited the moment I shared the video. Other classes needed time to think through Theresa's request.

Once a few interesting thoughts were thrown out as possibilities, I started to see the students' minds reel with ideas and excitement. I set specific guidelines for the rhythmic composition to ensure student success without limiting their creativity.

We created the final product, the method book, in Google Slides using the Flat for Docs add-on. Google Slides allowed for small-group collaboration, and the Flat for Docs add-on enabled each group to embed music notation in their slides. (More on how to use these tech tools in Chapter 11.) When all the slides were completed, we shared the document with Theresa to use with her students.

Activity Desctiption: (Offer step-by-step instructions)
1. Show the rhythm on the board
2. Let the students study and pratice on instruments
3. Hand out instruments (Four differnt drums, two drums for two people, hand out maracas and tambourines.)
4. Play

Insert rhythm exercise here:

Students created an ebook of rhythmic activities for peers in another state, which gave greater purpose to a rhythmic composition project.

I had more evidence of student learning than years past. I had time to visit small groups and meet their needs in the moment, as I could better understand their areas of struggle and mastery. The students had more time to get feedback and use it before completing the project, creating a more reflective process and in-depth learning experience. Not to mention that it's a project they remember being so fun to create!

A Few Notes on Music Composition

We believe that students should perform their compositions, whether that means performing for a friend, the entire class, or even an outside audience. It's important for them to connect what they write with what is heard. This will vary with the type of composition project they're completing. For a quick composition activity, having them play for a classmate may be enough. In other circumstances, with more elaborate composition projects, you might even orchestrate an entire event to showcase student compositions.

Depending on the structure of your music class and your teaching style, you might ask your students to play or sing something before notating it, and this is okay. There are many philosophies on which should come first, notating or performing, and we don't suggest that one is better than the other. We believe there's a time and a place for both. Consider your musical goals and teaching style when making this decision.

The type of notation you use will depend on your students and the available materials. Notation doesn't always have to use pencil and paper. Many teachers will have students compose using whiteboards and dry-erase markers. For young musicians, rhythmic composition could come in the form of Popsicle sticks, Play-Doh, Beat Blocks (more on this tool at the end of this chapter), or other craft supplies. This eliminates the need for precise fine motor skills that can sometimes be a barrier for successful notation. We should teach traditional music notation, but only when developmentally appropriate.

Digital music notation is also an option. Between the availability of student devices and the ease of use of the programs, this has become very simple to incorporate in school music classes. We love using Noteflight with our students (more on that in Chapter 11), though there are many options available. Once again your musical goals will determine when it's the right time to incorporate digital notation for composition projects. If you want students to work on drawing music notes correctly, digital notation is not the best choice. If you want them to have a polished final product, then it might work better than anything else.

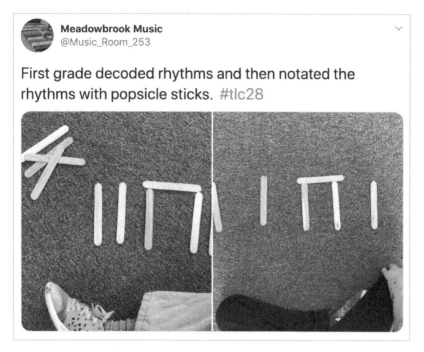

Meadowbrook Music
@Music_Room_253

First grade decoded rhythms and then notated the rhythms with popsicle sticks. #tlc28

Students notate rhythms with Popsicle sticks.

Finally, keep in mind that we should not limit music composition to classical styles and traditional notation. Think about what musical styles best fit your learning goals for the class and are relevant to the students. This could include anything from songwriting to hip-hop, electronic music, and more. When students are empowered, they take ownership of their music-making and develop a connection between the music and their own lives.

How-to Videos

Now that digital media and 1:1 devices are so prevalent, it's very easy to find tutorial how-to videos for just about anything. Many teachers assign students to watch a video as a reminder of a technical skill, for an additional explanation, or to learn more advanced concepts. And when possible, have students create these videos!

Having students think through the process of teaching others is powerful. First, the student must have a thorough understanding of the skill or task and the steps necessary for completing it. Then they must be able to verbalize and demonstrate those steps. In the terms of Bloom's Taxonomy, this takes them from simply remembering a skill or technique to understanding and applying it.

For example, first-year violin students can create videos teaching how to hold a violin bow properly. But they first have to understand how to hold the bow properly themselves. Next, they must explain each step, where each finger belongs, using the correct terminology to describe the parts of the bow. By creating the how-to video, they're able to demonstrate their learning and show a deeper understanding of the skills.

Students enjoy this opportunity to be the expert, and they appreciate being able to create content similar to what they so often consume. In turn, it's a means of formative assessment for us teachers. By watching these videos, we can determine which students understand the skill and which ones still need more reinforcement.

You can use student-created how-to videos in almost all settings. Students can demonstrate skills or techniques on an instrument, teach how to read or analyze music, or even teach a lesson on music history. Vocal music students can demonstrate and teach vocal warm-ups, describing both how to do them and why they're necessary. In some situations, you might assign everyone the same video topic; in others, you might give students a choice in what they want to teach. This will depend on your musical objectives for the project.

Consider using a tool like Flipgrid (discussed further in Chapter 11) for easy video creation and sharing. Other tools such as iMovie, WeVideo, or even the camera on a phone or tablet will work just as well.

Makerspace

Makerspaces are becoming more and more common in schools today, but many don't realize they have musical applications as well. A makerspace is a collaborative learning space, typically found in a school, dedicated to hands-on creativity. Often these spaces are filled with craft materials and recycled objects such as cardboard, Legos, blocks, and crayons—but they can also include some high-tech items such as 3D printers, coding tools, microphones, recording programs, and more. Within a makerspace, students are encouraged to explore, learn, make, revise, and reflect—all the things we want empowered music students to do. As music teachers, we can use makerspaces to meet a number of different goals.

If students are learning about instrument families and how various instruments produce sound, you might have them complete a makerspace activity building an instrument. You could have them make a new instrument, then demonstrate to the class how it produces sound and explain which family of instruments it belongs to. In a makerspace with tech tools, students might have the opportunity to experiment with recording and DAWs, or even be able to code their own instruments using simple computer science programming language. Sometimes makerspace projects have specific, teacher-directed goals (such as creating an instrument), while other times students may just be given the chance to play and create on their own. (More coding projects will be discussed in Chapter 11.)

A makerspace doesn't have to be a formal station in your classroom, nor need it be something that's used on a daily basis. If your school already has a dedicated makerspace, it might be worth inquiring how music students could also benefit and have opportunities to create in this way. However, don't get stuck on an actual space in your school or classroom. Collect materials when needed for an upcoming project, put them on a cart in your classroom, and voilà—a makerspace on wheels!

Classroom Materials and Decorations

How many of us have posters in our classrooms detailing musical notation, terms, or other types of information? We'd guess most teachers do,
but how many of us have given students the opportunity to create these
posters, or at least determine what we display and where? Probably not
as many. If we're displaying things in the classroom to help students
(information they'll be consuming), shouldn't they have some say in
what goes on the walls?

Theresa: Joy Kirr, in her book *Shift This!*, suggests having students decorate the classroom walls, or at least one portion of
the classroom. Inspired by Joy's idea, I tried this with my
fifth-grade band students. I asked for volunteers to decorate one of
the bulletin boards in our classroom. They had complete control, and I
had no idea what to expect. In all honesty, I imagined random pictures
and music notes. I sure was wrong! Instead, they created an interactive
board containing definitions other students might struggle with, practice suggestions, and QR code links to videos for more help! WOW! I
gave them the opportunity to create something for our classroom, and
they did a great job.

Student-created bulletin board

Having students decorate a music classroom can be tricky. We may have hundreds of students walking through our classrooms each week! This could result in many different messages on the walls, to serve the various audiences. If that's the case, look for one space in your room that could be given to a specific group of students—a bulletin board, a corner, or even the side of a file cabinet. Then determine who will get to decorate. You could assign a different class each month or quarter, or reserve the privilege for the oldest students you teach. Determine if the students will have free rein in their creations or if there's a specific theme or concept they must stick to. Regardless of what you decide, students will appreciate this opportunity to create and take over a part of the music room.

Creating for Recruiting and Promoting

When students create classroom materials, they're not exactly creating music, but they're creating for the purpose of the music classroom, gaining a sense of ownership. The same is true for having them create for the purpose of recruiting and promoting—where they take ownership of the music program.

Most music teachers who direct ensembles have to recruit during the year, and most who host events and concerts will at some point have to promote. Consider allowing students to take part in this process. They're capable of creating concert posters, either by hand or digitally, and they could create promo videos or commercials for upcoming events. In fact, using the "trailer" feature in iMovie makes this task very easy and fun! Taking a cue from Keith Ozsvath in Chapter 4, for instance, they could create individual videos in Flipgrid, inviting families and friends to a concert.

Older students could create videos or similar materials to help recruit others to participate in the music program at their school. The student leadership in a marching band could create a recruiting trailer to show incoming freshmen. Or middle school chorus students could create videos encouraging incoming students to sign up for chorus. Often students are our best recruiters!

Mandy Hollingshead, a music teacher in Beijing, has her beginning band students create a group TV commercial "selling" their instruments to incoming students. The students include factual information about their instruments and create a jingle for the commercial that they play on those instruments. Everything else is open to student interpretation. Having students share why they love being a part of the music program is likely to encourage other students to join. In turn, your own students have created something, again taking ownership of their music program.

Coda

With any project that students are creating, remember that guidelines are still necessary. They should know what the expectations and criteria are—even better, pass the baton so they can give input on both. Have a class discussion before a creative project to give them more ownership. Avoid too many limitations. Give advanced students the opportunity to use their skills and knowledge in a meaningful way. If all of them are creating the same product, question if you've provided guidelines or a recipe. While copying was part of the critical consuming-to-creating process, it's important to push past this stage and encourage students to create using their own voices.

When giving them opportunities to create in music class, consider starting with empathy and creating for others. Knowing someone else will see our creation is a powerful motivational tool for learning. When students create for other people, they not only share their past learning and the current creation but also learn so much about themselves along the way.

Next time you plan a lesson, rehearsal, or unit, take a minute to think about what your students are consuming and creating. Ideally, have a mix of both.

Things to Try Tomorrow

♪ Incorporate an improvisation exercise into your warm-up.

♪ Place a handful of rhythmic flash cards on the board and have students build rhythmic compositions using an elemental form such as abac abba abab

♪ Ask students to compose an original melody incorporating a specific concept or technique you have been learning about.

♪ Have them create a short video showing what they know about the recorder, the ukulele, etc.

♪ Have them create a soundtrack to accompany the narration of a story, either using instruments or technology. Make this a cross-curricular activity by working with the ELA teacher to use a story that those students wrote.

♪ Ask your students to create a poster advertising your next performance or event.

**Continue the conversation:
share what you tried with
#PasstheBatonBook!**

Encore: Beat Blocks with Abigail Blair

Abigail S. Blair is a pre-K–5 general music teacher at Westmoor Elementary School in Northbrook, Illinois, who offers many opportunities for students to learn through play. She strongly believes there is great value in giving her students time to discover, make mistakes, and try new ideas on their own. As they experiment and play, she has time to observe and check in on their learning. She believes students feel valued when they're set up for success and tasked with creation. Taking time to step back and let them explore, create, and share their discoveries is a vital part of the learning process!

Abigail found that giving students time to create with no guidelines was often crippling for them; there were too many choices, and they weren't prepared to create like an expert. Instead, she works to provide support and guidelines with just the right amount of challenge to push them to think forward. Small-group work where students can manipulate the learning with their hands and see musical concepts visually helps them find great success.

To this end, she created Beat Blocks: large Mega Bloks with music notation. Using Beat Blocks, students can discover and investigate rhythm, melody, and harmony, all within the guidelines determined by the music teacher. Visually, they can see the duration of note values, pitch relationships, tonal centers, and how harmonies can be created. Not to mention that Beat Blocks are an engaging way to create. When given time to work with rhythms on Beat Blocks, students can see and feel how those subdivisions work together within a measure. Students find it very easy to dictate or compose a rhythm because the blocks either fit together or they don't. They discover that there are multiple answers when composing. Guiding their choices with specific rhythmic notation leaves them free to create and discover with no chance for failure.

Abigail frequently uses Beat Blocks to work on rhythmic composition. Students get a set of Beat Block bases to represent the meter and measures, along with a variety of note values appropriate for them. In small groups they create their composition and share in a variety of ways, such as clapping their creation, performing on classroom instruments, or using a DAW or notation software. With careful instruction, Abigail can personalize a set of Beat Blocks for each small group of learners, giving them the "just right" experience.

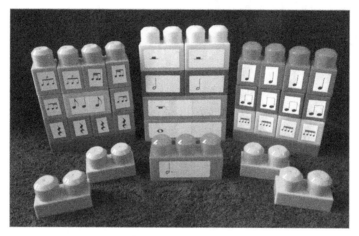

Rhythm Beat Blocks

Abigail created Beat Blocks so she could put learning into the students' hands. So much of music is aural, so the more ways she can make music tactile and visual, the better. While she still needs to prepare students with a basic understanding of rhythm, melody, and harmony, there is no need for a lecture. She finds value in small-group work, where her students can share their findings with others and build what they know with their new learning: "Students experienced an 'aha' moment when they discovered the duration of each note and how those subdivisions work together within a measure. This process of exploration, discovery, and creation is the center of the creative process."

Connect with Abigail!

♪ Website: www.buildingmusicalminds.com
♪ Twitter: @AbigailSBlair
♪ Email: beatblocks@icloud.com

7

The Empowered Music Student Asks Questions

Knowledge is a habit. Sometimes there's a limit to having new ideas. That's the problem with the old schooling. Because they were teaching answers. I believe that questions are probably more important today than the answers.
—Ernő Rubik, founder of Rubik's Cube

The important thing is not to stop questioning.
—Albert Einstein

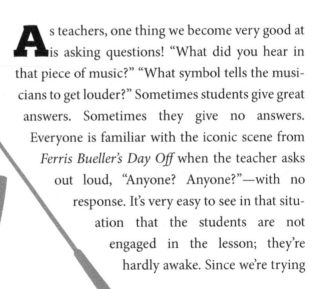

As teachers, one thing we become very good at is asking questions! "What did you hear in that piece of music?" "What symbol tells the musicians to get louder?" Sometimes students give great answers. Sometimes they give no answers. Everyone is familiar with the iconic scene from *Ferris Bueller's Day Off* when the teacher asks out loud, "Anyone? Anyone?"—with no response. It's very easy to see in that situation that the students are not engaged in the lesson; they're hardly awake. Since we're trying to take things one step further toward student empowerment, questioning techniques need to shift as well.

When we question something, we tap into our own curiosities. Picture your social media feed. Inevitably at some point you've seen a clickbait headline that makes you immediately stop scrolling. Before doing anything, you question. "What does this mean?" "Could it be true?" "But how?" Your brain needs to know the answer! You likely click on the headline to satisfy your curiosity and answer your own questions. This is inquiry in its simplest form. So how might we provoke student curiosity to ask these same questions about music?

How might we provoke student curiosity to ask these same questions about music?

Young children are naturally curious, frequently questioning all areas of the world around them. As music teachers, we can work to help them maintain their curiosity by incorporating inquiry in our music classrooms. Imagine if the next time you introduce a new (and especially, unusual) instrument to a group of students, instead of describing and naming it, you place it in the middle of the room. Let them look at it, walk around it, maybe even touch it. But you say nothing. They will be curious! They'll wonder, "What is this? What does it do? Does it make a sound?" After an adequate amount of time has passed, stop them and begin your discussion. Allow them to ask their questions. See if anyone knows the answer, an if not, share what you know with them. If you don't know the answer, show how you might find it. This experience will be much more impactful than if you stood in front of the room and simply described, say, the shekere, a West African percussion instrument.

According to Heather Wolpert-Gawron, the author of *Just Ask Us: Kids Speak Out About Engagement*, "Inquiry-based learning, if front-loaded well, generates such excitement in students that neurons begin to fire, curiosity is triggered, and they can't wait to become experts in answering their own questions."[1] During listening activities, ask students what questions come to mind when they first hear a particular piece of music. Or when learning to play or sing a new piece of music, encourage them to come up with questions about it first. Any way you can get them thinking and wondering about a topic before introducing it will make it valuable. Trigger their curiosity and get them excited about making music!

By allowing time for inquiry, you've added novelty, curiosity, and exploration to a lesson. John Spencer, in his book *Empower*, states, "Students should question answers as often as they answer questions." When they can both ask and answer questions, they've taken learning into their own hands, and their level of engagement skyrockets. While questioning and inquiry will look different in an elementary school music room versus a high school music room, purposeful implementation will benefit all students involved.

Wonder Wall

It's understandable that you may not be able to spend every day allowing students to ask all of their questions and discover all of the answers. Anyone who teaches younger grades knows how quickly one question can lead to another and another. Before long, you've fallen so far down the rabbit hole, there's no getting back on track! There is a solution to this challenge. In the book *Inquiry Mindset*, authors Trevor MacKenzie and Rebecca Bathurst-Hunt suggest creating a "Wonder Wall" or "Inquiry Corner" where students can post their wonderings or questions.[2] In our case, these would be music specific. The Wonder Wall should be somewhere easily accessible so students can add questions and wonderings anytime.

After creating your Wonder Wall or Inquiry Corner, give the students time to investigate the answers to their questions. One way to do this is by occasionally saving ten minutes at the end of class and dedicating it to answering questions. You could also make the Wonder Wall a station that students rotate to during class, using that time to engage with and explore the various wonderings.

You may need to guide the research of younger students, or even have sources prepared ahead of time. You can curate resources using a tool such as Wakelet, or have the students conduct their own internet search through the school library website or a kid-friendly research site. For older students, demonstrate using the Google search settings to filter by date and source type or to enable the Safe Search function. Common Sense Education (commonsense.org) has great information about this topic.

When you model the inquiry process and make your own thinking visible, your students learn how to do their own inquiries safely and accurately. Web literacy is a skill all students and musicians will need for their future. Older students may work independently in small groups to research and find answers. Sometimes research will come in the form of experimentation, and we should encourage this! Any way that students can explore and learn more about what makes them curious is valuable. While reserving time for this might feel excessive, your students will benefit and appreciate the opportunity to have their voices heard.

Theresa: When I added a Wonder Wall to my elementary band and orchestra room, I placed a bulletin board by the door. I provided Post-it Notes and a pen so my students could quickly and easily add their questions to the board. I'll admit, I added the first "wondering," hoping to fuel the fire. Within a few days, several students had added their own thoughts!—insightful questions like "Why are band instruments made of metal?" and "Is a string instrument louder when played arco or pizzicato?" After the next concert, we took some class time to explore their questions and discovered answers!

A Wonder Wall, placed on a bulletin board in a music classroom

Designating a day to research and discuss their Wonder Wall questions, after a concert or before a break, works perfectly. Also consider a day when you frequently lose class time because of shortened periods or assemblies. Taking the time for inquiry instead of showing a movie or giving a study hall is worthwhile. The level of excitement you can achieve will surprise you!

Genius Hour

"Genius Hour," or "20-percent" projects, take Wonder Wall questions to the next level. In a Genius Hour project, students are given class time to work on a project of their choosing. This concept did not begin in education, however. It started in business. 3M, a company well known for their office supplies, first introduced it in 1948 by giving employees 15 percent of their workweek, approximately six hours, to focus on an idea of their own. While many innovations came out of this opportunity to experiment and wonder, the most recognizable is Post-it Notes.[3]

More recently, Google has become known for allowing employees to work on 20-percent projects, where they use that portion of their workweek to explore a project of their choosing. This has resulted in products such as Gmail, Google News, and AdSense.[4] For Google employees, these projects are typically things that fall outside of their given job descriptions, but are ideas they're interested in and passionate about.

In the music classroom, Genius Hour projects can take many forms. An hour is not required, nor is it limited to 20 percent of students' class time. Instead, look at the time you have and decide based on what is best for you and your students.

For a Genius Hour project, students are first encouraged to come up with an essential question. Essential questions are "un-googleable"—a simple Google search cannot answer them. These questions could connect to a specific topic—a time period in music history, musical instruments, composers, etc.—or be left open to any musical interests students might have. By leaving it open, you help them connect the class standards and objectives to what happens beyond the walls of the classroom. This is when learning becomes most powerful!

Sample essential questions:

♪ How did the orchestra change over hundreds of years?

♪ How do composers write music for video games?

♪ How do you play the ukulele? Where did the instrument come from?

Throughout the process of the Genius Hour, students must determine a plan for their learning and then carry out the project. Opportunities for reflection are frequent. Genius Hour concludes with them creating a method to showcase their learning. This showcase can be done in any way meaningful to them—a video, a classroom display, a podcast, or a performance. While the demonstration of learning is a valuable part of Genius Hour, having them work through the process of asking questions and finding their own answers is the most important piece.

Genius Hour projects empower students in many ways. They are given voice and choice, the opportunity to create something, the opportunity to ask and answer their own questions, and a way to own the learning process. When you're setting up a Genius Hour, think about the parameters that work for your class. Maybe you can dedicate a few class periods after a concert to this work, or one period each week for a month. It's important that you allow students enough time to choose a project, fully engage with it, create a demonstration of learning to share with an authentic audience, and then reflect on their learning. Attempting to rush through any part of the process will only cause frustration for you and them.

After experiencing Genius Hour, both students and teachers will have had a glimpse of what inquiry looks and feels like. It helps us shift our instruction more frequently to allow creativity and collaboration to take place.

Brainstorming Sessions

Brainstorming sessions are great for engaging a large group of students. Many ideas are generated; organized, and ranked to help create next steps in the creative process. By brainstorming, you model your willingness to take risks, and you offer students the chance to ask questions and find answers.

A brainstorming session can take place in several settings. A high school band director might engage students in a brainstorming session when planning the next year's marching band show, or a middle school show-choir director might have students generate choreography ideas for a performance. Students can brainstorm the parameters for any upcoming project or an approaching field trip.

Encourage your students to think in questions, incorporating both broad and specific thoughts in their wonderings. "How could we put a pirate ship on the football field?" "How could we surprise the audience in the middle of this piece of music?" "How do we ensure that everyone has fun during the performance while remaining safe?" By framing thoughts as questions, you avoid concrete ideas and encourage room for creativity in and around the thought. Students will often dig deeper to the root of the challenge or task when they're asking questions. They may feel less self-conscious asking a question as opposed to offering a specific idea.[5]

Remind them that when you're brainstorming, no ideas are too large or too small! Once you've compiled all the questions, determine as a group which are worth pursuing further. Some will require further research; you can add others to the "save for later" or "discard" list relatively quickly.

You can brainstorm in an elementary school general music room as well. Kathryn has her fifth graders ask questions and find answers when planning for their spring musical, which they're all required to be in. Some students prefer to sing in the chorus, others love to be on stage, and still others find their place working behind the scenes with lights and sound. However they participate, the process begins with a read-through of the script. They break into small groups, and as they read, they wonder and brainstorm ideas for each scene. Through Google Classroom, they share a document to house their wonders and ideas.

Kathryn always reminds students that the document is a list of ideas they're brainstorming. Due to time, money, resources, and safety concerns, not all ideas will make it. As students brainstorm, they look for connections between ideas and for manageable suggestions, and together they come up with next steps for the musical.

Some may ask if it wouldn't be easier to take the lead and direct the musical yourself. While yes, it may be easier, you'll find this is much more rewarding. Students take ownership of the production. They participate more during rehearsals and have fewer attendance issues. Not to mention that the look on their faces when they see *their* wonder unfold on stage is precious. This process takes more time and may be challenging, but it's so worthwhile.

Some students might spend more time changing the background of a slide or making silly comments on the shared doc. They're getting off task and letting you know they aren't engaged. They need more structure and support from you. But many others will amaze you! They'll think of things that never occurred to you. Fifth graders who learned how to play the ukulele in music class suggested finding a place in the musical to feature them. Once they found a meaningful place for the ukuleles, others decided how they would perform the pieces. For another scene, they had prisoners in a brig, and students questioned how they could make this appear more authentic.

One student created the lighting effects while others found background music to set the mood for the scene. Another student asked what the artwork should be on the playbill. Then he researched sample playbills and created his own. They were happy to coordinate their efforts and thrilled to see their questions turn into solutions that materialized on stage.

Structuring a brainstorming activity like this in small groups allows you to meet your students where they are. They come with a variety of skill sets. It's rare that they inherently know how to work in a group and how to share ideas with others, and yet collaboration, critical thinking, creativity, and communication are vital skills for their futures as musicians and in life. The beauty of instruction like this is that you're free to provide support and structure for some, while stepping out of the way for others who don't need you.

Please understand, we do not step aside and let students run the musical from beginning to end. For fifth graders, this would not be a wise idea. We plan and pace our rehearsals to make sure the production is a success. However, when we incorporate ideas into our production from the brainstorming sessions, we give credit to the students responsible for the work. They beam, and their classmates cheer.

Coda

According to an article in the *Harvard Business Review*, "People with higher curiosity quotient are more inquisitive and open to new experiences." In addition, people who are curious generate more original ideas and better manage complex tasks.[6] For musicians, these are all desirable skills! When we can ask our own questions and find our own answers, we open our minds to new experiences that push our thinking and musicianship forward. If we stay where it's comfortable, we fall behind. Learning never stops.

When thinking about making time for questions and inquiry in the music classroom, remember your goal from Chapter 1. What do you want for your music students? What do you hope they'll gain from their time in your classroom? What do you want your students to ultimately remember and take away? Most likely it extends beyond what occurs in the classroom—beyond elementary music class, intermediate band, middle school orchestra, or high school choir. Encouraging your students to ask their own questions and explore their own curiosities about music will help them gain independence in their learning. They won't rely on you to continue their journey as musicians.

Things to Try Tomorrow

♪ When introducing a new piece, have students listen to the music and then come up with their own list of questions.

♪ Give them a class period (or even ten minutes) to explore something they've always wondered about.

♪ Create a Wonder Wall or Inquiry Corner for them to collect their questions and wonders.

♪ Allow them to brainstorm questions—as a class or in small groups—about an upcoming event or performance.

Continue the conversation:
share what you tried with #PasstheBatonBook!

Encore: Genius Hour
with Amy Rever-Oberle

Amy Rever-Oberle, the band director at Hart Middle School in Michigan, has all seventh- and eighth-grade band students ask their own questions and complete a Genius Hour project following their spring concert. Each student chooses his or her own musical objectives, drawing on their own background, interests, and curiosities. Some use what they've learned in band to come up with a project, but others find something they have no background in at all. Students work on their projects in class, dedicating a few periods each week to the project for about one month. At the conclusion, they present their projects in a gallery walk that other classes, families, and administrators are invited to attend.

To receive full credit for the project, students must meet the following requirements:

- ♪ For seventh graders, the project needs to relate to music somehow; for eighth graders, it should have a fine arts focus.
- ♪ They must blog about their progress (a minimum of six posts).
- ♪ They must seek an outside expert/mentor.
- ♪ They must share their learning in a gallery walk.
- ♪ They must complete a self-reflection survey after completing their projects.

Amy agrees that this project demands a different role from the teacher. Instead of presenting information, she spends most of her time checking in with her students and networking on social media to help find mentors for them. Often she will model the process by working on her own project, her biggest being a QR code inventory system for band instruments.

While initially administrators were concerned about students remaining engaged and on task throughout such an unstructured project, those feelings quickly dissipated. Some students required an occasional redirect, but most were actively engaged throughout the process. On their reflection surveys, nearly all said they enjoyed the project.

When asked what advice she would give other music teachers interested in trying a Genius Hour project with their students, Amy warned that many students will initially struggle with the open structure and lack of a rubric. They want to know how to get an A. You can eliminate that concern by giving them bigger items to check off (the project must relate to music, they have to create a blog, etc.) to earn the A. Even if a student's project flops, the experience can still encourage them to take more risks instead of going with the safe idea to get the good grade. Teachers must be okay with saying, "I don't know" and encouraging their students to look and learn elsewhere for the help they need. Also, be okay with some chaos. Engagement will look different for each project. As long as your students are safe, let them make a few messes and some unstructured noise. Amy found inspiration in Don Wettrick's book *Pure Genius* and online resources by Joy Kirr.

Connect with Amy!

♪ Email: amylynnrever@gmail.com
♪ Twitter: @amylynnrever
♪ Blog: thenoisyroomdownthehall.blogspot.com

8

The Empowered Music Student Is Connected

We live in a time where we have unlimited access to information in our pockets, but more importantly, we have unlimited access to one another.

—George Couros

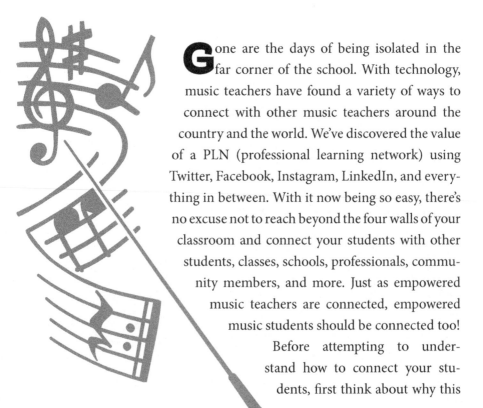

Gone are the days of being isolated in the far corner of the school. With technology, music teachers have found a variety of ways to connect with other music teachers around the country and the world. We've discovered the value of a PLN (professional learning network) using Twitter, Facebook, Instagram, LinkedIn, and everything in between. With it now being so easy, there's no excuse not to reach beyond the four walls of your classroom and connect your students with other students, classes, schools, professionals, community members, and more. Just as empowered music teachers are connected, empowered music students should be connected too!

Before attempting to understand how to connect your students, first think about why this is important. From a general education standpoint, we can see that by connecting students to those outside of the classroom, we provide them with an authentic audience, digital citizenship practice, and the ability to build practical skills. Specifically, as musicians, these practical skills include being able to appropriately interact with other musicians, directors/teachers, and audience members, not to mention knowing how to be a good audience member. These are not skills we can overlook.

Connecting students outside the classroom can help them find more purpose in their music-making. Going back to Daniel Pink's writing, people need to believe their work has purpose and value. Rarely in our world do we do work in isolation. Connected students see their music-making as part of the world outside the school and therefore make more personal connections with it.

In a world where artificial intelligence caters to our own interests and opinions, it's even more important to seek other perspectives. We can learn so much from others. Creating music is a personal experience, and when we share our music, we share a piece of ourselves. By teaching students to respect someone else's opinions, culture, and perspective when making music, we are teaching empathy. To again quote the *Harvard Business Review*, empathy is one of the "essential ingredients for leadership success and excellent performance."[1]

When we share our music, we share a piece of ourselves.

We should note that while many techniques and ideas mentioned in this chapter will revolve around connecting digitally, face-to-face or in-person connections are just as powerful! Never discount the opportunity to bring a live expert or live audience into your classroom. Many of the preparations will be similar, and these live connections can build an even greater sense of empathy.

Digital Citizenship Skills

Some would argue that only a tech or media specialist should teach digital citizenship skills, but we respectfully disagree. This is something we all can teach, and teach in context, so students see its importance in the moment. As musicians, we need to know how to share our work online—what is legal and what is not. We must understand the rights others have to their own music and the circumstances where using that music is appropriate and allowed. We need to know how to speak and interact with other musicians—student or professional—online. We also need to know how to react when someone responds questionably to us online.

This does not have to be a separate lesson; in fact, it's more authentic when naturally incorporated into what you already do. Students do not inherently know the do's and don'ts when online. It's up to the adults in their lives to give guidance in this digital world. When you model these skills, they see what a professional, positive digital footprint looks like and how they too can create an online presence for themselves, both musically and otherwise.

Today, we can collaborate with others in different parts of the world with ease. But our students need support through this process so that they see themselves as empathetic digital citizens who have value to share with the world. When they gain this knowledge and these skills, they have tools to help them take control of their learning and their music-making.

Give and Receive Feedback

Connecting with others outside of the classroom asynchronously (meaning, not taking place at the same time) gives you the opportunity to coach students in appropriate interaction before there are immediate consequences. If you watch a video of another group performing, what comments should your students make? When is it appropriate to give criticism? How can they do this constructively? What if someone says something a student disagrees with, or performs a piece differently from the way they would? And what is the best way to accept criticism? Learning these things is definitely part of becoming a better digital citizen, and these are also such important life skills! By coaching students asynchronously, you give them the tools to react positively when the interaction takes place in real time.

In the general music classroom, we work with students on how to give constructive peer feedback. Often we'll have each class in a grade level prepare a piece for a buddy performance. Prior to the performance, we'll record the piece and solicit feedback from other classes in the grade. This way we get to use the feedback to improve our performance for our buddy class.

Peer feedback is a powerful learning tool, and it is necessary for continued growth. However, students don't always know how to give constructive feedback. To help them, we'll often provide sentence stems such as "I liked how . . ." or "I wonder . . ." At the beginning of this process, as a class we'll offer feedback to another group using a digital document that holds the performance video and all comments made by peers. A tool such as Padlet works well for this. As teachers, we model comments first using the sentence stems. We might say something like "I noticed the group had a strong entrance to their performance. I liked how they had a student leader to conduct the ensemble. The introduction really caught my attention. I wonder if the student conductor could give a cue at the end of the performance. This might help the ensemble finish together with a strong, impressive ending." Students then choose one of the provided sentence stems to contribute their own feedback.

We're better now at stepping out of the way. When our students brainstorm feedback to give to another class, we write word for word what they say. We let them discuss the feedback, and then we offer edits and suggestions. Often we want to fix the wording or soften the language, but doing this takes the learning opportunities away from the class. The open discussion allows them to learn from one another and edit their work together. We guide them when needed, but only after they've had a chance to discuss and work things out among themselves.

Sometimes they make mistakes. Comments aren't always constructive or received well when you begin this process. Develop a safe environment where risks are encouraged, feedback is valued, and reflection is key. Sometimes students give weak feedback, such as "I like your melody." While it's nice to hear people like your work, the feedback isn't specific enough for reflection. Of course, some children just want to hear "I like your melody" and feel criticized when someone offers constructive feedback. Helping them give and receive feedback develops over time with great care.

The reality is that they will come across poor or even hurtful feedback and comments in their life. This can even happen when adults are supervising. While under our care, we can help them work through what to do when they come across an inappropriate comment, or what constructive feedback looks like and how to receive it. When students make a mistake and respond in a way they shouldn't, we can teach them why their response is not appropriate and provide a strategy for giving constructive feedback next time. And we can help those who are sensitive to any feedback to see how necessary it is for improvement and growth. As we've said, students are navigating a digital world daily with little to no support. If we can help them learn to give and receive feedback, it will help them grow as musicians and as online citizens.

An Authentic Audience

On the home page of his website, Rushton Hurley writes, "When students know that others will see their work, they want it to be good. When it's just for the teacher, they want it to be good enough."[2] How true is this statement? When students are performing something for the teacher, *good enough* will suffice. But when they're performing for the entire class, the school community, or even strangers, they want to make sure it's *really good*! And this isn't something only our students do. We all react this way. We strive to be great teachers, for example, every day, but many of us will step it up a notch when being observed by an administrator or colleague. This is a natural human reaction, and it's okay. It also opens the door for us to capitalize on the phenomenon.

Think about an authentic audience you could have students share their music-making with. Students in another school? Families? Community members? Professional musicians? Giving them an audience outside of the typical school environment encourages them to look closely at their music-making and ensures it meets the standard they'd like the world to see. It also encourages them to make decisions based on the needs and interests of their audience, providing a greater value and purpose to their work.

Connect with a Composer or Professional

There was a time when teachers were hesitant to admit they didn't know the answer to a student's question. Teachers were expected to be an authority on all topics in the classroom, and music teachers were no exception to this rule. Luckily this is no longer the case. We're not suggesting that teachers stop earning their "highly qualified" status, or do less work when preparing lessons, studying scores, or practicing their instruments. But they should be willing to admit that they're not an expert in every aspect of their music room and be okay with that. In fact, modeling to your students the importance of seeking expertise when needed is a valuable lesson for them. That's when bringing an expert into your classroom is beneficial.

With technology like Skype and Google Meet, this is easier to do than ever. We can connect to others from around the world with nothing more than an internet connection and a webcam. Why not make this happen in your classroom as well? Think about a lesson you teach: How could that be enhanced by inviting an expert into your class?

Consider asking a composer whose piece you are working on to provide a clinic during a rehearsal, or a member of a professional ensemble to give a master class. There may be someone in the music industry who could talk to your students about what that career path looks like. The only limit to whom you can contact lives within your own creativity and willingness to spark a conversation. You'll find that many people will help for free or a small fee, or at least point you in a good direction to look. If you feel uncomfortable reaching out to a stranger, consider asking a friend or a colleague in another school first and offer to return the favor and speak to their classes. Any kind of outside perspective can be beneficial to your students.

Theresa: My fifth-grade band connected with band composer Scott Watson via Skype when we were preparing his piece "Super Hero" for our spring concert. Two weeks before the concert, we had Dr. Watson "join" our rehearsal. We spent half of the rehearsal working on the piece and the other half in discussion with Dr. Watson. The students prepared questions in advance to ask him. They enjoyed learning more about his process for composing "Super Hero," and music composition in general. One student was especially excited when he answered her question about how to get started composing by pulling his notation sketchbooks off the shelf to show the ensemble. She came to rehearsal the following week with a composition notebook of her own, already containing ideas!

Composer Scott Watson connects via Skype with the fifth-grade band.

Having this authentic audience and knowing the composer would hear their music made my students even more excited to master the piece. They didn't want it to be good, they wanted it to be great! Having Dr. Watson listen to the piece elevated the experience beyond what they would get from a typical spring concert performance. Learning from the source of the creation gave them a higher appreciation and understanding of the work. As they listened to him talk about his creative process, they were able to see music composition at work in real life.

Social Media

As we've already discussed, having your class connect on social media is easy to do and opens the door for them to have an authentic audience and practice their digital citizenship skills. Social media gives the world a window into your classroom. Other music teachers and their students can connect with you, not to mention the transparency it provides to both parents and administrators!

When students know we'll share their music on social media, whether Twitter, Instagram, or a private Facebook page, they understand it will be viewed by a much wider audience. You can discuss what is worthy of sharing and why. They can practice drafting posts that explain their learning or describe the music being performed. They might even enjoy working as a group to create a response to another music class they've connected with.

Social media is a great place to look for those other classrooms to connect with, or even professionals in the music industry. We've found musicians and teachers on Twitter to be especially open to these ideas and eager to connect. When you're first exploring social media, follow as many educators and musicians as you can. We can learn so much from one another! While connections might not occur immediately, eventually you'll discover possibilities you weren't even aware existed.

It's a good idea to ask your students for permission before posting their pictures or videos on social media—this is assuming you already have permission from the parents and the school. We must be respectful of their feelings and privacy. While most students are excited about this opportunity to share and connect, some would rather not. We allow those students to put a sticker or emoji over their face in a group picture, or they may even act as the photographer so they can take part without being photographed. By asking them for their permission, you strengthen your relationship with them and build trust. In addition, you model good digital citizenship, teaching them to do the same when they consider posting pictures of friends and classmates.

Before jumping into a class social media account, there are a few things to think about. In the US, most social media networks require users to be thirteen years old to register for an account. This is in accordance with the law that prohibits collecting personal information from children under thirteen years old without parental consent. We are not suggesting you have students create social media accounts, but instead that they are included on your school account. To do this, you must have the school's and the parents' permission to post pictures or videos of students and their work.

Many school districts will obtain parent permission at the beginning of the year for students to be photographed and named in yearbooks, on the school website, in print media, on social media, and in other mediums. Parents can opt out of any or all of these, depending on their preferences. Check first with your administrator to see if this permission has been granted. Additionally, many schools ask teachers at the beginning of the year which (if any) social media accounts they plan to use. Investigate all of this before you get started. If there's a teacher in your district who is great at connecting through social media, consider asking them for suggestions on where to begin. This may save you some work in the long run and help you feel more comfortable when getting started.

If you don't have permission to post photos or videos of students, there are still options. Consider taking pictures from the back of the room, only photographing the backs of students' heads. Alternatively, there are several "blurring" apps and similar tools available that can make student faces unrecognizable. Or take pictures of the materials used in the lesson or a student's project (if given permission). Regardless, be sure to know your school's and the parents' policies before taking the plunge into any social media. Better safe than sorry in this situation!

Connected Classrooms

Connecting students to other students can be a very meaningful experience for all involved. While the internet and social media have opened our eyes to what goes on in other parts of the state, country, and world, to truly connect with those students is a very different experience. As humans, we're naturally curious about other people, so why not give your students the opportunity to learn from their peers?

In the past, we connected classrooms and students as pen pals. Theresa remembers a multiyear friendship with her European pen pal beginning in third grade. While pen pals may or may not still exist, we can connect students and our classrooms easier than ever. Think of something you're working on with your class that would benefit from having other students involved. Is there a piece you're performing that you'd like your students to see how others interpret? Or are you learning about music from another culture, and can you find students who could share this music firsthand? Maybe you have younger students who would enjoy the experience and guidance older student musicians can provide. Or you may even have older students who could act as mentors and help with retention for younger musicians.

Theresa: I've connected ensembles with other groups working on the same piece. In one case, my orchestra was working on the well-known beginner piece "String Explosion" by Frank M. Rogers. Through the Facebook Orchestra Teacher's group, I found another teacher whose ensemble was working on the same piece. Throughout the semester, we sent each other biweekly videos of our progress. My students would watch the video of the other ensemble, have a quick discussion about what they noticed, and as a class, craft a response including words of praise and suggestions for polish. The other ensemble did the same for us. Both groups were fascinated by watching each other work and progress. They were empowered by the experience of giving peer feedback, as it required them to think critically about what they saw and heard and respond with empathy when giving their thoughts.

The Ensemble Recording Exchange is another example of connecting classrooms for ensembles. Interested music directors can search a database to find a school to exchange recordings and feedback with. From their website: "This is a great way to reach more standards involving critiquing performances, using musical terminology, communicating via speaking/listening or reading/writing, and using digital tools. We hope to provide school ensembles the opportunity to provide feedback to other student musicians on music they are familiar with."[3]

Kathryn: Connecting classrooms can add purpose and value to creating musical compositions. Remember, in Chapter 6, when I asked Theresa if she would help me motivate my students to create a rhythm book for her students? Through email and Google Slides, we could connect classrooms across the country and stir up a lot of empowered learners. We worked on this project for the last few weeks of school and, for some classes, up to the last day of music. In fact, on that day, I planned singing games to play with the kids. To my surprise, a handful of them asked for a laptop to make last-minute tweaks to their Google Slides. They were so invested in the project that they wanted to work on the last day of school!

Theresa's students had three more weeks of school before summer, so she had time to try a few exercises with her students. She reported back that they had fun exploring the book and loved having something so personalized to do before summer vacation. When school started again, I had students asking on the first day of music, "Well, did they like our method book? Did they use it?" It made me realize how deeply invested they were in this project.

Connect Students Through Flipgrid

Flipgrid is a great tech tool to connect students and encourage social learning. Using Flipgrid, students can contribute videos to a shared grid, learning and being motivated by one another as they go. When teachers set up a grid, it's a "walled garden"—only those with the code can access it. As a result, students can safely share and connect with a variety of audiences. They can connect with other music students in the district, share their learning, promote upcoming events, or even create videos for recruitment. Younger students can connect to an older mentor student, creating an asynchronous teaching platform where the older student provides musical guidance and feedback.

 Theresa: One of my favorite activities to facilitate with Flipgrid is our annual Holiday Music Grid. This grid connects students from schools around the country who all contribute videos of holiday music. They play band and orchestra instruments, sing, play the piano, and one even performed "Jingle Bells" on the zither, taking the time to introduce the instrument and its history. Students are motivated by hearing the various songs played, often pushing themselves to learn more difficult music. Frequently, my younger students come to class begging for the sheet music for pieces they heard older students playing. They're also very supportive of one another.

Older students leave video messages for younger students, encouraging them and congratulating them on achievements. Younger students show admiration for their older peers and the work they do musically. What started as a way for them to share holiday music turned into a beautiful celebration of musical voice, inspiring students from all ends of the country to practice, learn, and connect.

In another example, Kathryn and I connected our classrooms on Flipgrid for her recorder unit. My fifth-grade band students learned to play the recorder in third grade and also learned to apply many of those skills—breathing, posture, articulation—to their band instruments. My fifth graders were offered the opportunity to connect with Kathryn's third graders and get them started on their recorder journey.

They all began by creating introductory videos. My students then recorded a series of videos explaining various beginning instrumental topics. Some even found their old recorders and taught specific notes and songs! Kathryn's students watched the videos, practiced the skills (supplemented by her own teaching as well), and then recorded videos of their progress. My students provided feedback and encouragement. Everyone bonded over music-making. Kathryn could have easily taught the recorder unit as she always did, but instead she connected her students to my fifth graders, who then became empowered as teachers. They became the experts!

Virtual Ensembles

When we wrote this chapter in October 2019, virtual ensembles were rare and in some cases frowned upon. Why would someone put together an ensemble virtually, knowing the power of in-person music-making? We still felt this was an important topic to include in the book, even though so few people were taking part and many did not see the value.

And then COVID-19 hit. Our lives as music educators transformed.

Suddenly, the hot topic from music teachers on social media became "How do I make one of those virtual ensembles?" Now we've seen "Zoom bands," multitrack choirs, and everything in between.

We questioned keeping this section in the book with everything going on in the world, but decided it needed to stay. The information is valuable, and the message is relevant. Connecting students through musical experiences is necessary to their growth and to help them become empowered. We know that now even more than ever! We can't discount what virtual and online projects can provide.

Eric Whitacre, conductor and composer, was one of the first to attempt a virtual ensemble, with his "Virtual Choir." Singers from around the world were invited to upload videos of themselves singing a specific song, which were then compiled into one performance. The experiment, first attempted in 2009, has grown into at least eight iterations featured globally. In 2013, Whitacre and the Virtual Choir collaborated with Disney to produce the song "Glow" for their *World of Color–Winter Dreams* show in the Disney California Adventure Park. The most recent (to this publication) Virtual Choir performance, "Deep Field," even gave participants access to an online forum to connect and share stories with other singers.

Anyone can create a virtual ensemble experience for their students. Levent Erdoğan, an Apple distinguished educator and digital media specialist, shared a project on Twitter in which he compiled videos of students playing "Star Wars" on their recorders. They learned to play the music from the tutorial videos on his website and recorded themselves playing the piece. Then he collected and compiled the videos on Flipgrid. Does a project of this caliber take work? Absolutely. Video editing skills and/or magic are definitely needed, but it's doable. To make a virtual ensemble most effective, have participants record their track along with a metronome, or provide a backing track to align tempos. The actual compilation part might be something that older students would really enjoy. Whatever way you choose to try this, know that you are empowering your students. By helping them connect to others, you are helping them share the music-making process in previously inconceivable ways.

Mr. Erdoğan ♫ 🎺 📯
@MrErdoganEDU

#PLN, help me connect #ElementaryMusic Ss around the world for an EPIC VIDEO of #StarWarsOnRecorder!!

Via @Flipgrid and my YouTube channel, Ss can learn songs and post vids here:
Flipgrid.com/StarWarsOnReco...

#musedchat #FlipgridFever #Recorder #PowerOfVideo #RecorderSymphony #edchat

👤 Amy Rever and 9 others

9:58 AM · Jan 11, 2019 from Sai Kung District, Hong Kong · Twitter for iPhone

Mr. Erdoğan invites music teachers to have their students participate in a "Star Wars" compilation video.

Coda

Connecting your students doesn't have to be elaborate. Consider starting with your own PLN; even having another teacher friend connect with your class can be powerful. Parents and administrators can serve as experts too. It never hurts to ask. In the end, know that you're providing your students with an authentic audience, teaching them digital citizenship skills (if it's a virtual connection), and providing a means for them to take more ownership of their learning and music-making.

Things to Try Tomorrow:

♪ Create a social media account for your class. Find other classes and music teachers to follow.

♪ Connect your class with a professional. Find a composer or someone knowledgeable about a topic you're studying and reach out to them.

♪ Connect your class with another class. Start with another music teacher friend or someone in your district.

♪ Check out the Ensemble Recording Exchange website to find an ensemble you may be able to collaborate with.

Continue the conversation:
share what you tried with
#PasstheBatonBook!

Encore: Virtual Ensembles
with Michelle Rose

Michelle Rose is a music teacher at North Carolina Virtual Academy. In this virtual environment, her students can participate in a variety of music classes, but she felt that one thing was missing: her students couldn't connect with one another while making music. To remedy this situation, she created a virtual band and chorus for them. She's found the virtual ensembles to be successful when they incorporate two factors: students practicing on their own using SmartMusic and then attending live rehearsals using Zoom video.

All students must have a SmartMusic subscription. Each week, they practice with SmartMusic, then submit a recording to her. Prior to rehearsal, she listens to all the recordings and uses that information to determine what they will work on together. During Zoom rehearsals, she gives instructions and conducts, and her students play their instruments or sing. By default, their microphones are muted, so they can hear her instructions, but can't hear their classmates playing (attempting to play together with microphones on would cause significant problems due to the sound delays). This requires her to pay close attention to visual cues: watching fingerings, breathing, and posture, to give appropriate feedback to them. Every few weeks, she combines the SmartMusic recordings in Audacity to get an idea of what the full ensemble sounds like.

Virtual ensembles also give virtual performances! Again using Audacity, Michelle combines the students' final recordings into one product. The first of these final recordings of the choir's performance premiered at the school's Virtual Art and Talent Show, and the band premiered a recording of "Pomp and Circumstance" for the school's graduation ceremony! Students were very excited to be part of these special events.

Michelle has found that rehearsals—and student collaboration—are the key to success for the virtual ensembles. Students will often join the Zoom rehearsal early to chat with one another and get to know the other members of the group. Throughout the rehearsal, she can also unmute students to encourage conversation and collaboration among them.

While she agrees that a virtual ensemble experience could never replace that of an in-person ensemble, she also feels strongly that this is an excellent solution when it's not possible to be in the same room. Participating in virtual ensembles has given her students a chance to be part of something and feel connected to other students in the school. This is often difficult to achieve in a virtual school environment.

"You don't have to be in the same physical location to get to know someone," Michelle says. Her advice to someone thinking about starting a virtual ensemble is to be open to making mistakes and learning alongside your students. There is definitely a learning curve involved with running a rehearsal in an empty room. She also recommends, for the first rehearsal, having a slide displayed with visual instructions for students to check their microphones and speakers. Inevitably at least one student won't be able to hear you, so this saves time in troubleshooting the settings that will need to be adjusted.

Connect with Michelle!

♪ Website: www.themusicalrose.com
♪ Email: michelle@themusicalrose.com
♪ Instagram: @the_musical_rose

9

The Empowered Music Student Owns the Process

Our job as teachers is not to "prepare" kids
for something; our job is to help kids learn
to prepare themselves for anything.
—A. J. Juliani

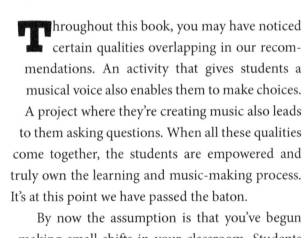

Throughout this book, you may have noticed certain qualities overlapping in our recommendations. An activity that gives students a musical voice also enables them to make choices. A project where they're creating music also leads to them asking questions. When all these qualities come together, the students are empowered and truly own the learning and music-making process. It's at this point we have passed the baton.

By now the assumption is that you've begun making small shifts in your classroom. Students are sharing their voices, making choices, creating content, connecting outside of the classroom, and asking their own questions. You may even find that in some areas they've already started to take ownership! This chapter will contain a mix of things that you can do as the teacher and your students can do for themselves, once they own the learning process.

Listen and Let Go

Letting go can be a challenge for many music teachers. As a conductor, Theresa definitely feels this way. Conductors are used to being in charge. It's their job to prepare and plan. They typically know the desired outcomes before the day begins. However, when you enable students to own the learning process, much of that changes. You will need to trust that they're ready for this responsibility. You need to prepare for the fact that some of them will make mistakes—and that's okay! If you've been working to empower your students so far, they'll understand that learning is messy, and that making mistakes, taking risks, and even failing are necessary parts of the process. They'll have the tools to reevaluate and try again. This is where the best learning happens.

Listen to your students. What do they want to do? What do they need from you? When you listen, make sure you truly hear what they are saying. Let go and allow them to take the reins. Your experience in the classroom and your relationship with them should allow you to know when it's time to keep control and when you can let go. Start small, establish expectations, and take a chance. If things get out of control, regroup and discuss with the students what happened. Then determine together what will lead to the best chance of success next time.

The Guide on the Side

Your role as a teacher changes in an empowered classroom. Your students still need you, but in a different, more personalized way. There's a common phrase stating that teachers move from being the "sage on the stage" to being the "guide on the side." This is completely accurate! Sometimes when the students in your classroom are working together, either rehearsing in their small ensembles, leading their own warm-ups, or collaborating on a composition project, you might stop and ask yourself: *What should I be doing? No one needs me!* That feeling only lasts for a moment. In no time there will be someone asking for your opinion on a melody they just created, or needing a new reed, or wanting to share their progress on the piece they're working on. And anyway, that feeling is a good one. It means your students are empowered.

At times you'll find yourself *advising* students as opposed to directly *teaching* them. You listen to them when something isn't working as planned or a group member suddenly has different ideas. You offer encouragement when the going gets tough and congratulations when a plan works out. While you might offer suggestions and feedback along the way, you and they both know the decisions are ultimately in their hands. As an advisor, you may point your students in a general direction, but you will rarely give them the direct answers they're looking for. Your role as the guide on the side is to steer them in their thinking, but not control their choices.

We believe that in many situations, students can figure things out on their own. This can be everything from finding the correct fingering for a note on their instrument to understanding why a composer notated the music a certain way. Sometimes we need to remind students about the tools they have to find the information they need. Other times we act as a sounding board as they work through a challenge. We've already empowered them to ask their own questions and find the answers, so they may only need encouragement or reminders.

Depending on the age of your students, you may need to take charge of all connections being made outside of the classroom. Younger students likely won't have email accounts and may rely on you for this task. That doesn't mean you do all the work, though! They can still craft their letters and responses to others. In some cases, when dealing with school officials, say, a request might bear more weight with a teacher's name attached to it—for example, if students are putting together an event at the school and they need to reserve space. Allow them to include your name on the request while still making it clear that they're the ones doing the work.

Theresa: During a Genius Hour project in my class, one student was very curious about movie soundtracks and how composers create this kind of music. He asked if I knew any film composers. While I did not, a request in the Music Teachers Facebook group provided us with the email address of a well-known film composer willing to answer some questions. My student wrote his letter in a Google Doc and shared it with me. I wrote an email to the composer, introducing myself as a music teacher and briefly explaining our project. My student's letter was copied below my introduction. The composer wrote back the very next day, giving detailed answers to all the questions and even included a link to preview one of his upcoming compositions! My student was thrilled. My role during this was simple: make the connection. It was my student who had the idea, determined where he needed to go to find answers, and made it happen.

Putting It All Together

Find something in your classroom your students can take complete control over. Or even better, ask them what kind of project they'd like to do. You might have specific standards or curricular requirements they would need to fulfill in the project—or you might give them control of that as well. Student-led informances and performances, project-based learning, and self-assessment are great opportunities for them to share their voices, make choices, create something, connect with others, and ask questions. When all of these factors are put together in one experience, they will have ownership over the learning process.

Student-Led Informances

In many elementary or beginning instrumental classrooms, informances are ideal ways to showcase student learning. An informance is an "informational performance." The audience is learning alongside the students. One benefit of an informance is that it focuses on a process, not only a finished product. This aligns perfectly with empowering students!

When an informance is student led, they're responsible for all the details: determining what content will be shared with the audience, how to demonstrate the process, and planning how the information will be conveyed. When Theresa taught beginning instrumental music, the first time students performed for an audience, it was an informance. They made a list of everything they could share with parents, voted on what to include, and wrote any necessary explanations of the process. While Theresa facilitated the conversation and took notes, they made all the decisions. During the rehearsals leading up to the informance, they had input on what they worked on each day and provided feedback for themselves along the way.

Kathryn: Before you think this is something only older students can do, know that kindergarteners are equally capable! Each year my kindergarten students perform in a spring music program for their parents. In the past, I would spend weeks preparing every detail of this program. Now I've given my students ownership over this process. A few months before the performance day, I ask them, "What are some activities we've done in the music room that you'd like to share with your parents?" From there we vote on the activities and put a program together. I create a slide show for each of the three kindergarten classes I teach so I can remember what the groups want to share. I also add the learning targets to the slide show for each song or activity. It's important to share student voices at the informance, so when we're rehearsing, I ask them, "What did we learn from this activity?" As they respond, I dictate word for word right into the slide-show presentation.

My kindergarteners are engaged in this entire process, and together we create an end product. With support from me, they can select repertoire, practice, and reflect on their work; personalize the program to their interests and needs; and make their thinking visible. They are excited to share this with an audience. After all, it's their creation!

Student-Led Performances and Events

Older students may take control of planning an entire performance or event. A student-run chamber recital is the perfect example of this. Students can choose and rehearse the repertoire, create the program, advertise, and set up the performance space. This takes place under the guidance of the teacher, but the students are the ones who make it happen.

This is also a place where they can connect their music-making to areas of their lives outside of school. Students with interests in nonprofit organizations might put together a benefit concert. Those involved with their church or community youth groups could find value in arranging a performance for one of those organizations' events. The real-world application gives their work an authentic audience that is truly meaningful to them. This is the type of experience that they remember for a lifetime.

During this process, you'll see students naturally gravitate toward different roles and tasks. Those who don't see themselves as musical leaders might have a knack for design and want to work on creating advertisements. Others who are aspiring music teachers might want to try conducting or leading their group. Encourage them to explore an area that interests them, but also to step outside of their comfort zones and try something new.

When students are working on larger performances and events, you can introduce project management and other useful skills. Most musicians have probably performed in groups that were well managed and groups that were not. We know how much this impacts our experience. Guide your students in how to distribute tasks between group members, effectively communicate, and stick to a schedule. These are skills we use regularly as musicians, and skills that will be beneficial in many other areas of their lives.

Project Based Learning

Project based learning, or PBL, is another excellent way for students to own their learning. The Buck Institute for Education's PBLWorks defines

PBL as "a teaching method in which students gain knowledge and skills by working for an extended period to investigate and respond to an authentic, engaging, and complex question, problem, or challenge."[1] Students work on real-world projects and demonstrate their learning with a product or a performance for an authentic audience.

Don't confuse PBL with "doing a project." Often when we think about doing projects in a class, the project is the result of learning. An example might be having students complete a composition project after learning about music notation. In PBL, the learning *is* the project! Students are learning the entire time they're engaged in the project. Our colleague and friend Melissa Dyas explains the difference this way: a project is like a ride at the boardwalk. You wait in a long line and eventually go on the ride. PBL is like a ride at Disney World: you're engaged in the ride experience from the moment you step into the line!

Like Genius Hour, PBL starts with an essential question that encapsulates what you want students to know and do. An entry event is used to introduce the project and "hook" the students. This could be a video, a guest speaker, or even a field trip. Students work through the project content primarily on their own, though mini-lessons and small-group instruction from the teacher can take place. The PBL experience ends with a public demonstration of learning, including an authentic audience.

For example, imagine a unit where students learn about the time periods in music history. The essential question might be "How can we characterize the various periods in music history in terms of the people, music, and outside influences?" You could introduce the project by Skyping with a music historian or exploring a music exhibit within the Google Arts & Culture website. Students could spend the next several weeks immersing themselves in music history, learning about different time periods, composers, genres, etc. The demonstration of learning could be a museum, created in the classroom, where a separate student group puts together an exhibit for each time period. Families, staff members, and other classes would be invited to tour the museum at the end of the unit. Throughout the project, students would learn the necessary information and create their exhibit and any additional resources to help a museumgoer.

Within this type of project, students are responsible for learning the content. The teacher may include basic requirements, such as including information about a specific number of composers or historic events, but the students can dive deep into areas that most interest them.

Project based learning also lends itself well to cross-curricular connections. A project such as the one described could easily involve the art teacher, having students learn about art history alongside music history. Or maybe a technology teacher would lend support in helping students create digital content in addition to the physical museum exhibits. Once again, the only limitation is your own and your students' creativity and willingness to connect with others outside of your classroom.

Self-Assessment

Student self-assessment should not be reserved for the end of a project or performance. It can and should happen in many areas along the way. Students taking control of this part of their learning is necessary for them to own the process.

As with peer feedback, we must first teach them how to self-assess. Many students will want to tell you something is "good" but will have nothing else to say about it. Start with something simple, like having them show a thumbs-up or thumbs-down for a performance, activity, or their understanding of a new concept. Another method is the "fist-to-five," where students show a fist if they felt something was no good, five fingers if they felt it was amazing, and any number of fingers if they felt something in between. With these methods, you're encouraging them to decide how they felt about something, but not requiring any descriptive content yet.

From there, you may move to having them assess areas of their performance using specific criteria or rubrics provided by you or from standard assessment tools. For example, those preparing for an audition may find value in assessing themselves using the same rubric the audition judges will use. Ensembles preparing for festivals or contests can do this as well.

Using open-ended questions will require students to think critically about their music-making. With that type of question there are no right or wrong answers, yet the students must think beyond a simple yes or no. Consider asking them to identify and explain specific areas of their performance that went well and areas that still need more work. They could also discuss what they worked hard on, or areas where they noticed the most improvement.

Part of their success in musical self-assessment comes from learning appropriate descriptive language. When providing feedback, do you simply tell them something was "good," or do you tell them what aspects were good and why? By training them to listen for pulse control, intonation, and tone quality, you're giving them more tools to use when they assess themselves. Unfortunately, words like "good," "nice," and "okay" provide little value to them. The more musically descriptive words you can use, the more they'll have available for their own use.

Ideally, with practice, they'll use this descriptive vocabulary to explain their assessment of something and have a conversation with you or a classmate about it. Find time to meet with them and discuss their assessments. Even if you can only do this two or three times a year, it's worthwhile. Allow them to see their self-assessment next to your assessment of their performance. Having a conversation about why each of you felt that way about the performance or project being assessed helps them learn and grow as musicians.

Ways to make self-assessment even more powerful:

 ♪ Have your students select the criteria and/or create the rubric.
 ♪ Have them create a reflection or assessment journal, to monitor their progress throughout the school year.
 ♪ Encourage them to come up with their own open-ended questions.
 ♪ Give them the opportunity to evaluate the work of others against a rubric. This will help them better identify quality work.

Coda

Owning the learning process is the goal for empowered music students. When they're comfortable expressing their opinions, making choices, creating, asking questions, and connecting with others, we have set them up for success in the future. They can think for themselves, make decisions, and understand the importance of the process, not just the product. As we've given students these opportunities to own their music-making, we can take comfort in knowing that we've helped influence the impact music will have on the rest of their lives. Not all of them will make music their careers, but all will find their personal connection to music and how it can bring value to their lives.

Things to Try Tomorrow

♪ Examine your role in the classroom. Find one place where you can move from being the "sage on the stage" to the "guide on the side."

♪ When preparing for an upcoming performance, find tasks that your students can take over, giving them ownership over the process.

♪ Explore the PBLWorks website for other ideas on how to incorporate PBL in the music classroom.

♪ Allow your students to assess themselves on their next performance task. Have them compare this assessment with the one that you also provide.

Continue the conversation:
share what you tried with
#PasstheBatonBook!

Encore: The Latin Musical
with Miriam Capellan

For several years Miriam Capellan, a pre-K–5 vocal-music teacher in Arlington, Virginia, has joined forces with her sister Liz Gephardt, a middle school Latin teacher, for a student-created musical. Liz's eighth-grade Latin students create the storyline and script based on what they've learned about Greek mythology. Miriam's fifth-grade students are the songwriters, creating the music they'll eventually perform. Originally, Miriam and her sister would write all the music, but more recently they've passed the baton to give their students this experience.

Miriam's main objectives for her students include tune creation and songwriting, as well as collaboration and performance. Going into the project, she gives them information about the purpose of the play, the plot, and any song lyrics the eighth graders have created. She helps guide them in finding an appropriate key for their vocal ranges, and she instructs them in a few basic ukulele chords to provide a framework for their initial improvisations. They form groups, and each group chooses which song or group of lyrics they want to work on. From there, Miriam takes a step back and allows them to explore their own ideas and inspirations.

She notices a variety of songwriting processes among her students. Some find it easier to not use the ukuleles and instead "tune doodle" in their heads. Others use solfège as a guide. Some gravitate toward the piano for help, while one group found their inspiration on drums. (She gently guided them to make their song tuneful and less of a chant.) The students use Flipgrid to record their ideas and remember their melodies. Having them work in small groups allows Miriam to circulate through the room, giving feedback and assistance as needed.

Students take ownership of the songwriting process, and as a result, they have greater ownership in the final performance. Miriam enjoys seeing some students who were apprehensive about singing in front of others later singing solos in the final performance. Having their ideas as the centerpiece inspires them to want to take ownership and communicate their artistic vision to the audience.

When asked what advice she would give to someone interested in taking on a similar project, Miriam says to take your time and be willing to follow the students' lead. The creation of tunes and songs can be messy and is a highly unique experience for everyone. At the start, it often feels like it will not work at all! It just takes a lot of trial and error to find a way that works for each student. Also, it's okay for students to take on different roles during a group songwriting project. Not everyone will contribute significantly to the final tune used in a performance, and that's okay. There are many other ways to be involved in the process!

Connect with Miriam!

♪ Twitter: @choralmiriam

Encore 2: Shenandoah Conservatory's ShenCoLAB

While most of this book has focused on examples from K–12 schools, we want to acknowledge that this work of student empowerment even extends into the university setting. Students at Shenandoah Conservatory, part of Shenandoah University in Winchester, Virginia, are given the opportunity to engage in student-directed projects as part of their innovative program, ShenCoLAB. Each fall, the conservatory cancels classes and rehearsals for one week, giving students access to facilities and resources to work on their own projects. At the end of the week, projects are presented on campus at their Festival of Arts, Ideas, and Explorations.

ShenCoLAB was inspired by similar programs at the Royal Welsh College of Music and Drama and Trinity Laban Conservatoire of Music and Dance, both in the United Kingdom. Conservatory faculty hoped that ShenCoLAB would enable students to work on projects that interested them and practice creativity, collaboration, and teamwork, as well as develop other skills that would benefit them moving forward in their careers. The ShenCoLAB gives students a chance to explore ideas within their fields that may not have otherwise been possible given available time and resources.

They begin by submitting proposals to indicate the scope of their project and needed resources and participants, as well as an explanation of their goals. While the projects are student led, faculty members can visit rehearsals and offer insight if needed. Student groups are responsible for determining who will lead the project, planning how the group will use their time and obtain needed resources, and carrying out the final performance.

The projects are varied and include a wide range of traditional and nontraditional performance elements. There are collaborations of music and dance, immersive theater performances, research-based lectures, ensemble performances, original compositions, and more. While there is a final product associated with the project, the focus is actually on the process and giving students a safe environment to explore all that entails.

In some situations, the project extends beyond the ShenCoLAB week. One partnership developed during ShenCoLAB continued throughout the school year as students discovered a passion for playwriting. The original project grew into a staged reading, which they are working to turn into a full musical production.[2] Another student recorded an album of songs and poems designed to help babies in neonatal intensive care units, which was later approved for use in the NICU in a nearby medical center.[3]

Connect with Shenandoah Conservatory!

♪ Website: https://www.su.edu/conservatory/shencolab/
♪ Email: ShenCoLAB@su.edu

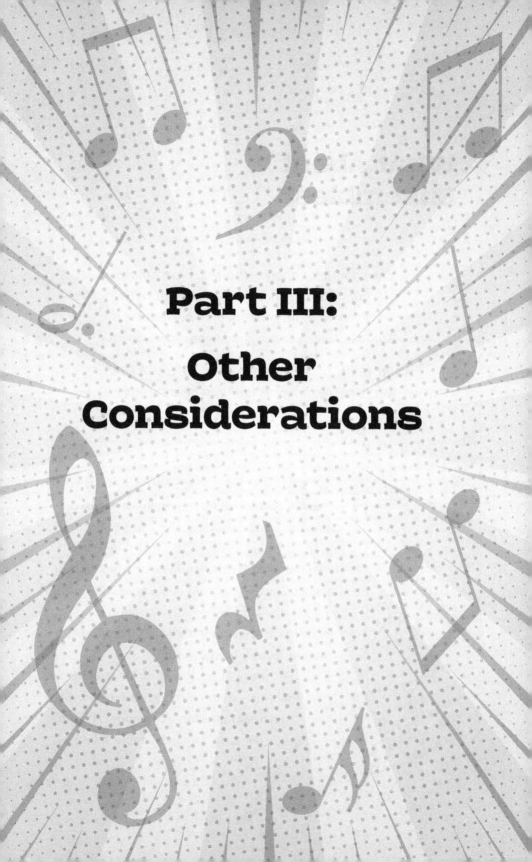

Part III:

Other Considerations

10

What About Ensembles?

The conductor of an orchestra doesn't make a sound. He depends, for his power, on his ability to make other people powerful.
—Benjamin Zander, Boston Philharmonic music director

A star wants to see himself rise to the top. A leader wants to see those around him become stars.
—Simon Sinek

Some say that a good leader doesn't strive to make himself look great; he strives to make those he leads look great. We can say the same for an ensemble director. The goal should not be for you to look like the world's best band director or choir director; it should be for your students to look like the world's best student musicians. Yes, for one to happen, most likely the other must also. But the focus is on the learners.

For many of us, the word "director" is in our title—choir director, band director, orchestra director, etc. Empowering students in large ensemble rehearsals will be more challenging, since they are by nature teacher directed. However, hopefully you've noticed throughout this book that there are still ways to empower students in these settings.

There is still a time and a place for a conductor! One thing that makes the most celebrated symphonies worth hearing is the way the musicians seamlessly blend their sounds, working together to create beautiful music. If the tuba player suddenly decides he wants to be heard (using his voice and choice), there will be problems! The conductor helps shape the music, balance the ensemble, and bring life to the composition. But even the best conductors know you can't dictate every beat, every nuance. Sometimes you need to get out of the way and let the musicians make music.

> **Sometimes you need to get out of the way and let the musicians make music.**

There will be places you cannot give your students a voice and a choice. For example, events that require you to perform specific pieces of music. Rehearsal etiquette is a must for productive musical rehearsals. Director-assigned seating may be necessary to achieve the optimal balance and blend. This is all okay. Last we checked, the violinists in the Philadelphia Orchestra didn't get to choose their chairs either. Understand that in a large ensemble situation, you may need to be even more creative when empowering student musicians, but this doesn't mean you shouldn't do it.

Student Leaders

Students of all ages love to be leaders, and starting them on this path at a young age is great. As mentioned in Chapter 4, after we've established classroom routines, we'll frequently have our students lead warm-ups in band and orchestra rehearsals and during group lessons. While they do that, we'll often join the ensemble playing various instruments or sit by those students who need extra support.

At first, they all need a model and to have clear expectations set. For example, in Theresa's beginning orchestra class, after they'd been playing the D-major scale several weeks in a row with a variety of techniques, she invited a student to lead the orchestra in playing the scale. The student came to the front of the room to lead the group. Some student leaders take to this role naturally, feeling comfortable and confident when standing in front of the group. These are the ones who try new things with the ensemble and aren't afraid to take risks. Others need more prompting from the teacher. You might have to say something like "How will the orchestra know when to start?" to remind them to cue the ensemble. Either way, it's empowering for the student.

After they've had more experience being leaders, allow students more freedom. Offer suggestions like "Lead the group using a song in the method book that incorporates slurs" or a similar skill needed that day. Other times it might be appropriate to be more vague, asking the student to choose a warm-up or exercise that would help with a particular piece of repertoire to be worked on later in the rehearsal. Their creativity might surprise you, and the ensemble will appreciate the change of pace. Another great time to use a student leader is when you have someone who's already learned a skill you're about to teach. Instead of teaching the concept yourself, ask them to do it!

Theresa: When my band students would learn about dynamics for the first time (we had experimented with loud and soft playing, but hadn't labeled terms yet), I asked a student who'd already learned about dynamic changes in her piano lessons if she'd like to teach it. I gave her a couple days' notice and asked her to plan a short lesson around the concept. She was great! She explained and demonstrated the basic dynamic markings, then had the ensemble play one of our scale warm-ups at various dynamic levels. The rest of the ensemble was attentive the whole time because they were curious what their classmate had to say. They were also supportive and appreciative of her effort.

It's easy to fall into the habit of only encouraging high-achieving students to take on the role of student leader; however, all students should get the chance if they are interested. You are meeting them where they are and helping them grow from that point. Expect there to be some giggles and restarts the first time you do this, but with time and practice, they'll take their role as the leader seriously and have the same expectations that you do.

Consider what additional strengths they might bring to the group. Do you have a student pianist who could accompany choral warm-ups or rehearsals? Could a student with photography skills take some artistic photos of the ensemble? We once had a student create an amazing visual presentation (using Google Slides) to project as we performed "A Prehistoric Suite" by Paul Jennings for a concert. In any of these scenarios, students are using the skills they have and are proud of to add value to the ensemble. When you give them these opportunities, they gain ownership within the ensemble.

Many high school ensembles already have section leaders in place—typically stronger musicians showing leadership skills. These positions are important and great for empowering musicians. We still recommend you try to give these opportunities to as many students as possible. There doesn't need to be a specific title attached, just the experience. The one downside to only relying on a student leadership team is that it doesn't include all students. Find ways for everyone to share their voice by creating an ongoing process for them to give feedback and make decisions.

Students of all ages can perform jobs within ensembles that will give them ownership and, as a bonus, make time for you to focus on other things that need your attention. For instance, student music librarians can do everything from distributing music to collecting and sorting returned music. Or supply managers can be responsible for maintaining the supply area of the classroom (valve oil, slide grease, drum keys, pencils, and so on). Social media interns can take pictures or videos during rehearsal and compose social media posts, which are then shared on the class page. Student historians can record one awesome thing that happens each class period. While some of these jobs are more necessary than others (we could survive without social media interns and historians), students love being able to contribute in this way.

Students wear lanyards to signify the jobs they perform during class.

Paul Solarz, the author of *Learn Like a Pirate: Empower Your Students to Collaborate, Lead, and Succeed*, has students take responsibility for day-to-day tasks such as taking attendance and distributing paperwork. An "absent-minded professor" helps absent students by filling out a form detailing what they missed in class that day. For an ensemble, this might look like having one student per section whom others can go to for missed music markings or other information.

The "recapper" will lead a class discussion detailing any homework and classwork that students must finish, and the "evaluator" leads an additional discussion about how class went and where there is room for improvement. These may not be daily activities in an ensemble rehearsal, but it's easy to see how students could benefit. Maybe someone could recap the practice assignment and any upcoming events on an ensemble website or Google Classroom page. Or one student per section could lead a two-minute discussion about how the week's rehearsals went and what areas to address next, then share that information with the director (or the entire ensemble) via Post-it or Google Form. The more ways you can involve your students in the rehearsal process, the better.

Score Awareness

How often do you allow instrumental music students to examine the score for a piece you're working on? In most situations, we hand students their part to a piece, and that's the end. They learn their part, but never really understand how it fits with the rest of the ensemble. Can you imagine an actor being given a script that only contained their lines? Not knowing the context would be very challenging. Yet we do this to our instrumental students regularly. They gain a limited awareness of other parts during rehearsal, but many may not really understand the full work unless they hear a performance recording.

Choral students have the advantage of seeing all parts in their music. If your students are currently aware of the other voice parts in their music, that's great! You'll have an easy time implementing some ideas suggested here. Other students may put a visual block around parts not their own, in which case they would definitely benefit from taking a more detailed look.

Consider having them begin with a score study of their own parts before even playing the piece. While listening to a recording, have them follow along reading their music. What do they notice about the piece? What questions come up from listening? They can share these observations either through class or small-group discussions, or by using a digital tool like Padlet or Google Slides. Have them examine their music and ask questions before hearing anything from you. This will encourage them to take ownership and look deeply at other music as well.

Students who are older or more experienced with inquiry would likely enjoy seeing an actual score. While providing an entire paper score for each student in the ensemble might not be feasible, they could all follow a digital score. Many publishers provide these online. You might also consider handing out two or three pages of the paper score to study and then discarding them immediately after, to avoid copyright infringement. Students could also gain insight studying a new piece of music with a classmate who plays a different instrument. They can compare and contrast parts, asking questions and learning from each other.

You might question if looking at a full score helps young students. The answer is a resounding yes! The first time we showed our fifth-grade students the score to one piece we were playing, they acted as if we'd shown them the *Book of Secrets* from *National Treasure*! They are naturally curious and will enjoy this experience. They can ask questions, think deeply, and form opinions. By allowing them the time to explore a new piece of music on their own, you help them gain tools to be musical without you.

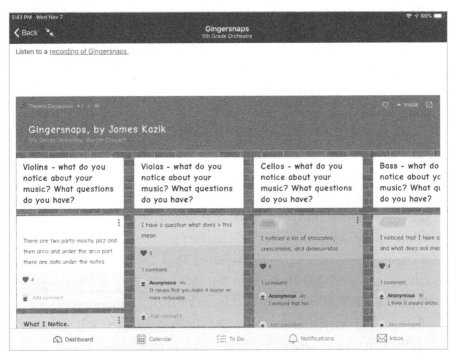

Student score study using Padlet

Student-Led Rehearsal Prep

After your students have studied a piece of music, either their own parts or the entire score, they're ready to think about rehearsals. Encourage them to identify specific challenge areas to address, asking if anyone has suggestions on how to rehearse them. At the end of rehearsal, they can reflect on their progress as individuals, or the progress of their section of the ensemble. You might ask them to suggest what sections should be the focus of the next rehearsal, so they can contribute to the rehearsal plan. If appropriate, you can use student leaders throughout this process.

If you think this sounds time consuming, you're right. It *will* take more time, especially at the beginning. But imagine the power of your students leaving rehearsal knowing exactly what parts of a piece need additional work before they rehearse again—not because you told them, but because they discovered it themselves. This isn't something you'll do for every piece or every concert. Instead, look for one or two opportunities throughout the year where it might be possible. When you give your students this opportunity, they learn more about the rehearsal process, understand more about the music, and develop their ability to own the music-making process.

Contests and Festivals

There are many varying opinions about festivals, assessments, and contests for musical ensembles. Our purpose is not to discuss the validity of these events, but to encourage you to think about what your students can get from them. Any event where they can receive direct feedback from an expert will provide more benefit than when only a number or rating is given. Find festivals that provide a clinic with adjudicators. We want our students to understand that knowledge and feedback can come from a variety of sources, and it's okay to look outside the classroom to learn more. By modeling a growth mindset when you receive feedback from adjudicators, you can show your students that you, the teacher, are always learning. This mentality will serve them well throughout their careers, whether in music or not.

If such an event doesn't exist in your area, why not start one? Begin with a few schools in your district or community. Take turns performing for one another. Invite a conductor from a local college or community group to give students feedback. As they connect with these adults dedicated to helping them grow and learn, students become more likely to seek similar experiences later in life. Consider having a festival before a public performance. This way your ensemble can implement some feedback for the final performance.

Self-Reflection and Goal Setting

Self-reflection and goal setting are important aspects of student empowerment. We've mentioned several times in this book how students will take ownership of their learning when they can articulate goals for themselves. This applies as well to ensemble settings.

Goals here should also be specific and measurable, such as determining a date to have a piece of music memorized. Throughout rehearsals, find ways to set goals *with* your students instead of *for* them. As an ensemble, reflect on recent performances, events, and even rehearsals. Students can look for what went well, what needs more work, and what factors contributed to both. This can be just as enlightening for you as the director! They might remind you that the last time you worked on a piece, the fire alarm went off, cutting the rehearsal short. Or maybe they'll explain that even though you taught an alternate fingering, they still aren't comfortable with it as required for a specific passage in the music. Allow them to make these observations and reflections on their own.

Nontraditional Ensembles

Many examples throughout this chapter and book have been specific to traditional ensembles, such as band, orchestra, and chorus. That doesn't mean, however, that the techniques and ideas suggested are limited to those groups. Nontraditional ensembles, such as rock bands, mariachi bands, a cappella groups, or any variety of ensembles playing popular music, not only benefit from but thrive in this environment. Having these diverse musical experiences available will help include more students who may not see the relevance and value that traditional ensembles provide.

Steve Giddings, author of *Rock Coach* and *Creative Musicking*, advocates that there are many benefits to students participating in rock bands at school. He's found that rock bands will engage those who might not otherwise take part in the school music program. They also offer enrichment opportunities for high-achieving students, provide ways for them to connect music to their personal lives, and promote creativity and independent musicianship.[1] This almost sounds like the silver bullet for student empowerment! Frequently in rock or popular ensembles the role of the teacher shifts from "instructor" to "coach," which is the same for classrooms where students are empowered.

Performance Opportunities

Finally, think about allowing your students to create some of their own opportunities to perform. Maybe one week, instead of giving a specific practice assignment, encourage them to find a place and time to give a performance. They could play for family members, neighbors, at church—or in whatever creative venue they can come up with! Do you have a group of students who have mastered their concert pieces several weeks in advance? Try letting them find and prepare a chamber piece on their own to perform at the concert. Require them to make all the creative decisions regarding the performance of their piece. Allowing students to take ownership of their preparation of the small ensemble is a great way to promote student ownership.

As the teacher, you may still want to guide and provide feedback along the way, but they should lead the process as much as possible. Many states and regions have solo and ensemble festivals where instrumental music students can gain performance experience outside of the traditional large ensembles. These festivals are often adjudicated, providing students with a rank, rating, and/or feedback on their performance.

If your area doesn't have these festivals, consider starting one, even if only for your own students. Ask a few friends or colleagues to serve as the judges, and invite high school or college students to act as guides at the event—you can possibly entice them with community service hours. Parent booster groups can be very helpful in organizing and providing volunteers. Interested students can sign up to perform the solo or small ensemble piece they have prepared. If you teach older students, you might even ask them to coordinate this festival for younger members of your district's music department.

Alternatively, you could create a more informal event featuring soloists or small ensembles. We've seen music programs set up a cabaret or coffeehouse evening in the school cafeteria, where student-led groups perform. Preparations for this event could take place during or outside of school, depending on your schedule, and students could take control of all logistics. They could add a fundraising element to the event, organizing a bake sale to support the school music program or collecting donations for a local charitable organization. When you allow them to take control, they can create an event most meaningful to their lives.

Coda

Throughout this book we've talked about numerous other ways to empower music students in ensembles. Give them choices in concert repertoire and skills assessment. Encourage them to create their own music, for themselves or for a small ensemble to perform. They can create personalized concert welcomes as Keith Ozsvath had his students do (see the "Encore" at the end of Chapter 4), or write program notes and piece introductions for concerts. Allow them to make musical decisions about a piece you're working on, as Derrick Fox does with his choir students (described in the Chapter 5 "Encore").

Keep in mind that when directing ensembles, our goal should be to teach music through performance. While having a strong performance is the objective, equally important is helping your students grow into independent musicians. Thinking back to your goals for your students, how can you best reflect that in your ensembles? Sometimes a teacher-directed approach is necessary, but look for opportunities to pass the baton. Both your students and your program will benefit.

Things to Try Tomorrow

♪ Ask a student volunteer to lead a well-known warm-up during rehearsal.

♪ At the end of rehearsal, ask your students to brainstorm two things to work on for the next rehearsal. Have them share these ideas in a class discussion or through a digital or paper exit ticket.

♪ Before they sight-read new music, have students list their own observations of what they see first.

♪ Encourage and support student-led small ensembles.

**Continue the conversation:
share what you tried with
#PasstheBatonBook!**

Encore: Student-Led Rehearsals in High School Band with Lauren Staniszewski

Lauren Staniszewski, the band director at Stoney Creek High School in Michigan, took a chance and implemented student-led rehearsals with her ensembles. At the beginning of the school year, she gave her students the opportunity to take ownership of the ensemble warm-up process. As a group, they discussed why warm-ups were important and how they could be most effective. Her students came up with a list of potential warm-up exercises and took turns each rehearsal determining the warm-up plan for that day. Once they were comfortable with that process, some even conducted the warm-ups.

What took the experience to the next level was when Lauren gave students control of an entire piece of music. She explained that they would choose a piece (from a preselected list), rehearse it, and perform it at the winter concert. She told them their goal was to "perform this piece to the best of your ability; to make it YouTube or social-media worthy, something that everyone at the end of the experience would be proud to share with their friends and social circle." Ultimately, her goal was for them to develop greater awareness and take more individual and collective ownership of their musical craft.

The first step involved class discussions to identify potential problems and roadblocks. Interestingly, her students were most concerned with trust and respect! Next they discussed how the rehearsals would work and determined what information they would need from Lauren prior to beginning. Finally, they voted on the piece they were to perform and established rehearsal norms. They were ready to begin practicing!

Lauren admits things were bumpy at first. After a time, the awkwardness subsided, and the students got into a flow. Once that happened, the experience became very worthwhile. She noticed they were problem-solving and having musical conversations. Engagement increased all around. They were holding themselves accountable and, as a result, running very effective rehearsals. "As a band director, I could not be any more excited that my students are not only concerned with how it *should* sound, but how they *want* their music to sound. Notes, rhythms, dynamics are not just answers to questions on a test—they are shaped into *art*."

In the end, all three ensembles performed their pieces with success at the winter concert. Lauren had found a way to have a positive impact on student learning, and she would definitely recommend that other ensemble directors try something like this. She found that by specifically addressing any challenges that might occur, as well as brainstorming solutions and objectives, the students could keep focus throughout the project. Her advice to other teachers wanting to try this project is to "be open and willing to take any teachable tangents the students present to the experience."

Connect with Lauren!

♪ Twitter: @LStaniszewski1
♪ Band website: schsbands.weebly.com
♪ Blog: cougarbandnotes.blogspot.com

Encore 2: Popular Music Ensembles with Steve Holley

Steve Holley is currently pursuing a PhD in music education at Arizona State University and is the former producer for the Commercial Music Program at the Kent Denver School in Colorado. Steve is an advocate for incorporating popular music in the music classroom, in an effort to reach every student. He has worked with popular music ensembles—including jazz, pop, R&B, Latin groups, and more—to give students ownership of the music-making process.

The first step for Steve was looking at his title. When he was working with students in a popular music setting, viewing himself as the "producer" rather than the "director" made a big difference. As the producer, he wasn't stuck in the front of the room on a podium. He could walk around the room, listen from different vantage points, and encourage his students to take the lead when suggesting how to improve a song.

Each student brings something different to the ensemble. Their varied backgrounds and musical experiences contribute to the success of the group. Steve found the popular music environment to be perfect for co-learning, where students have and create knowledge *with* the teacher as opposed to the teacher passing on the knowledge to them. He would frequently incorporate student mentors, pairing upperclassmen with lowerclassmen, or even high school students with middle school students. As a result, there was an increased sense of community and ownership.

Steve encouraged students to choose most of the tunes they would work on (with his guidance and precurated Spotify playlists). Each band was responsible for its own marketing and promotion, creating announcements, posters, and social media campaigns. Bands even came up with their own set lists for performances. While Steve would plan each rehearsal, often his students ran the rehearsals by counting off tunes and giving one another feedback. He felt it was important to let them learn from their mistakes instead of trying to jump in and direct. It's their band.

He found increased musicianship among them. "Playing in multiple styles of popular music helped my students to better understand music as a whole, as well as the social, cultural, and historical underpinnings of the music. They're also able to communicate in a number of styles of music literacies beyond, but inclusive of, standard notation." Additionally, playing in popular music ensembles has helped students connect their in-school music experiences with those out of school.

For someone thinking about adding popular music ensembles, Steve offers these thoughts: "Immerse yourself in the music, learn a new instrument, become a student again, play along to the radio, join a band, figure out ways to communicate through music other than notation. Get off the podium, put down the baton, give up control of the rehearsal, let the song fall apart, take the focus off the director, let the students have more say in the music, the rehearsal, and the performance. In other words, step back a bit and give up a little control here and there, scaffolding all the way. It might take years to change the culture, but when it does change, the results—when the students take ownership of their songs, their rehearsal, their band, their performance—are remarkable!"

Connect with Steve!

♪ Website: SteveHolleyMusic.com

♪ Twitter: @SteveHolley_

11

The Role of Technology

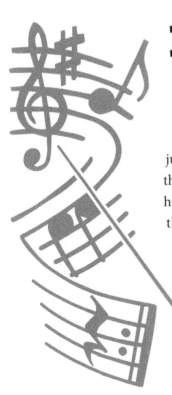

Why Use Technology?

Integrating technology in the music classroom and in our music ensembles is a topic that has many publications, opinions, and debates attached to it. Our belief is that technology can be a great benefit to music education, but it must serve a purpose. We should never use technology just for the sake of incorporating it. A great analogy that rings true as a homeowner has to do with the hardware store (we can't remember who first shared this, but if it was you, thank you!): When you need to fix something in your home, you go to the hardware store and select the tool that will help you complete that project. You make sure you've found the tool that's exactly right for the job. It's always a bonus when you can use that tool for future projects! What you don't do is walk around the hardware store looking for a cool tool

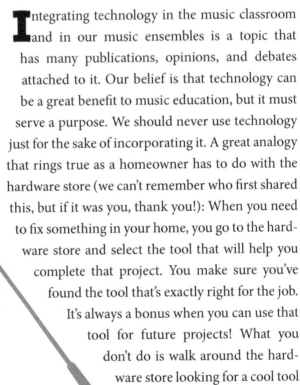

and then try to decide what to build with it. The purpose should come first, then the tool. The same is true with technology in music education. First figure out your musical goal and what you are trying to teach. Then look for the tech tool that will help accomplish that goal.

Our students are digital citizens. They don't know a world without the internet or cell phones and other smart devices. As educators striving to empower them, we would do them a disservice to not incorporate technology in their school music experiences. Technology can help them understand how music fits into their lives. While hearing a symphony play might not resonate with some, learning about composition techniques in video game music might. They may not feel a connection to composing a pentatonic melody until they can turn it into a ringtone for their cell phones. Technology can help make music relevant. No longer will students ask, "When am I ever going to use this?"

Feeling heard is a universal human need. Giving your students the chance to share and be heard is important to their learning experience. Technology can help you to recognize and amplify each student's voice and provide feedback asynchronously. Technology provides students a safe place to share their voices. As music educators, we see many students in classes and ensembles. How do we make meaningful connections with them when we see so many of them? Technology tools can be a great way to help us connect.

Technology can give students more choice, whether it's choice in how to show mastery of a skill, how to learn something new, or what music to learn. They might find comfort in technology options because they will be using tools they're familiar with or have used in the past. Technology can aid us as we move toward a more personalized approach in education.

There are many tech tools that enable students— from the youngest to the most advanced—to create music. Technology has made music creation something that truly anyone can do, and many tech tools have redefined what our students can compose. With these tools at their fingertips, they can learn to compose with great success.

Technology connects us to people beyond the four walls of the classroom. Music students can now connect with educators, professionals, community members, and even other students around the world. Sometimes they'll need support from an expert. Other times they may benefit from collaborating with peers from another state or country who can offer a different perspective. Connecting and collaborating with people outside the school walls builds empathetic students who know how to work with others and who value a different perspective.

In the elementary school setting, modeling these connections with an expert—guiding and preparing students to speak to others—sets a strong foundation for when they're older and can seek these opportunities themselves. Many older students already have a social media presence but little guidance or adult supervision for it. We as educators can and should model appropriate, positive interactions using social media tools and other technology so they see beneficial, responsible ways to use these tools at their fingertips.

Think back to the example in Chapter 3, the student who used YouTube to teach herself how to play "The Pink Panther" on the violin. At only nine years old, she took ownership of her music-making. She knew what her goal was, found the appropriate tool, and made it happen. With a growth mindset, musicians can crowdsource many desired skills at their fingertips. How do you restring a ukulele? Where can I buy a new case for my instrument? How do I play this chord progression? Students can empower themselves and give themselves the permission to determine the next steps. Of course, we're there to guide and support them, but if they have the motivation to find more information and try new things, they should!

This chapter will contain descriptions of broad categories of technology and specific tools, along with applications in a variety of music classrooms. These are only suggestions. There is no limit to what you can do as long as you think about the purpose of your lesson and what you want the technology to accomplish. It would be impossible for us to share all technology tools that could empower music students—this book would need weekly updates! But we've showcased the tools that we use most frequently, the ones that have the biggest impact on our students and appear to be the most timeless options.

Remember, when adding technology to a music class, we should not replace something we can just as easily do live or in person. We should use technology to create an experience that would not be possible otherwise.

Tools for Creating

Digital Audio Workstations

A digital audio workstation, DAW, is an electronic tool that enables the user to record, edit, and produce audio files. There are several digital audio workstations available, including GarageBand, BandLab, and Soundtrap. With these tools, students can create their own music! They can create ringtones, intro and outro music for YouTube videos, and various other musical compositions without the need to understand all the intricacies of music theory. They can find great success and focus on an appropriate level of music theory for their needs while creating a very satisfying, complex composition.

Most DAWs will include premade loops that students can use in their creations. Loops are short musical snippets that repeat, like an ostinato. Students can layer or combine loops in a variety of ways in their compositions. DAWs will give them access to virtual instruments that can be "played" within the app. In addition, they can record their own music, either vocal or instrumental, and incorporate it into their compositions. Having this wide variety of loops and virtual instruments to choose from gives students endless possibilities in their music creations.

Ideas for use:

- ♪ Students can create backing tracks to accompany simple songs that are either sung or played on instruments.
- ♪ They can create backing tracks to improvise over.
- ♪ They can create their own ringtones.
- ♪ They can record themselves performing a song and mix that with loops or other tracks.

Incredibox

Incredibox is a fun tool for creating your own music. The app and web versions allow students to manipulate a variety of "beatboxers" and layer ostinatos. Students can interact with the loops, record their own pieces, and share their creations on social media. Incredibox is simple for young learners, requiring them only to drag and drop the various elements. Older students can use critical thinking skills when analyzing their compositions and the various musical elements contained within.

Ideas for use:

- ♪ Define the term "ostinato" and layer many ostinatos, identifying each layer as melodic or rhythmic.
- ♪ Create a song as a whole class.
- ♪ Have the class learn about form and phrasing, then put students in small groups to create, record, and share.
- ♪ Have advanced vocal groups create a piece using Incredibox and then re-create it with their own voices.

Incredibox beatboxers

Noteflight (Digital Music Notation)

Noteflight is an online music notation tool accessible for music students of all ages. It's a web-based application you can use on most devices. Students can create and listen to their music anywhere with Noteflight and even have options to print and share with others. One great feature for educators is the Noteflight Learn platform. Within Noteflight Learn, teachers have their own websites where students can access Noteflight in a secure environment. The platform integrates with Google Classroom and several other learning management systems to easily facilitate distributing and collecting assignments.

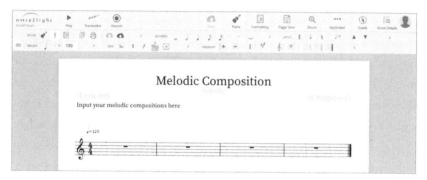

Noteflight, a digital music notation tool

With digital notation tools, students can create their own music compositions, see the professional-looking manuscript, and hear what the piece will sound like! Digital notation can empower them and provide them with the tools for owning their music-making process. Those who might have been limited by their penmanship, musical vocabulary, or knowledge of music theory have more avenues to create when using digital notation. Just as screen readers and dictation functions on computers aid learners when they're reading text, similar features in digital notation tools can help them when they're reading and writing music. Students wanting to write for a group have the benefit of hearing the piece even if the performers aren't all present. Getting this feedback, what the song accurately sounds like in real time, is empowering.

The Noteflight Learn teacher dashboard

Another great feature in Noteflight Learn is that it gives students the ability to record themselves playing along with a score or piece of music. They can even manipulate the tempo or change the key. They can also connect and collaborate within the class, creating a safe and controlled online platform to discuss their compositions with their teacher or classmates, or work together on one composition. They're creating music, using their voices, making choices, and connecting with others!

Here are some ideas for empowering music students using Noteflight:

♪ Provide them with a melody, either for voice or instrument, and have them add expressive elements.

♪ Provide them with a melody and ask them to create a harmony or bass line to accompany it.

♪ Have students create a song including musical elements studied in class, such as specific pitches, rhythms, expressions, or form.

♪ Have them create a melody for their instrument (within specified guidelines) and then perform and record the melody.

♪ Have them create a melody or song for someone else to perform. Connect them either in real time or asynchronously to discuss what worked and what they could adjust to make the piece even better.

♪ Have them create their own theme and variation on a melody they're working on.

Coding

Coding has become more and more common in schools of all levels. Many states and school systems have added computer science standards and also graduation requirements in this area. As music teachers, we can incorporate coding in our classes to continue our work of empowering students by improving creativity, problem-solving, persistence, collaboration, and communication.[1] These are all worthwhile skills!

In many coding activities, students can create musical experiences through trial and error while problem-solving and making creative decisions along the way. Coding offers them choice in what they create, how they create it, and how complex or simple the code is. They're using valuable future-ready skills in a musical setting. It's a win-win situation.

There are numerous coding platforms available of varying complexity, along with online resources and lesson plans for coding in music classes. Your school might already have access to one or more of these platforms. A conversation with your school technology teacher can provide ideas on how to incorporate these fun tools into your classroom and open the door for a great collaborative experience.

Coding Tool	Description
Makey Makey makeymakey.com	An invention kit to turn everyday objects into touchpads.
Scratch scratch.mit.edu	Block coding language created for students aged eight to sixteen. Scratch can be used with most web browsers, on computers and tablets.
Korg littleBits Synth Kit littlebits.com/ products/synth-kit	Assemble electronic circuits to explore sound, create instruments, and more. Includes a project book to get you started.
Specdrum sphero.com/ specdrums	A color-sensitive ring the user wears on his or her finger. The ring is connected to an app that allows each color to trigger a different loop or sound.
Osmo playosmo.com/en	Game-based block coding for students aged five to twelve. They use a phone or tablet attached to an Osmo base and reflector. Using the "Coding Jam" game, they can compose their own music.
Dash and Dot makewonder.com	Robots you can program with block code. A xylophone kit is also available to code music compositions.
EarSketch earsketch.gatech.edu	A website that teaches students how to code through music composition using coding languages Python and Javascript. The website provides a library of loops and sounds that the programmer learns to use and code to make their own music.
Sonic Pi Sonic-pi.net	Live music coding. Program sequences to create songs.

Kathryn: I needed to create adaptive instruments for students at my school. For some, strumming on a ukulele isn't an option, while for others, singing in the Winter Sing is not an appropriate goal. However, not participating or being excluded from these school experiences isn't okay with me. So, with the help of the special education teacher and some ideas from other music educators, I started coding my own adaptive instruments to meet my students' specific needs. With minimal coding experience, I can program sounds, connect the interface to a homemade button or trigger, and have a custom adaptive instrument!

An adaptive recorder, created by coding a Makey Makey

After I had success creating a few adaptive instruments, I realized my students could do this too. I gave my fifth graders a class period to explore the Makey Makey, an invention kit for turning everyday objects into touchpads. Using the Makey Makey website with a precoded piano, students could test objects to see if they conducted energy. If the piano makes a sound, the object conducts energy and can be used as a touchpad. Students then spent another class period learning how to code their own sounds using Scratch.

I tasked them to work within small groups to create adaptive instruments for classmates to use during music classes and the Winter Sing. Each group determined what instrument to create, identified a user, drew a prototype, and created a list of needed materials. After all the adaptive instruments had been created, we invited other classes to come to the music room and try them. My students learned what worked and what they should fix, and they spent the next class period making revisions before we gave the instruments to their intended users. By watching others try the new adaptive instruments, my students learned what was intuitive and what was not. As a result, they added directions or labels to their instruments to help. If they noticed too many wires were in the way, they redesigned the instrument to eliminate obstacles. Anytime the adaptive instrument was in use, I recorded a video so I could share this success with the fifth-grader designers. The amount of passion they had for this project was simply amazing, and seeing classmates use their creations was very gratifying for them.

Ideas for incorporating coding activities to empower music students:

♪ They can code instruments to play basic melodies or create their own original composition.

♪ They can code rhythmic patterns or loops to accompany a live performance, or their coded melody.

♪ They can code a robot to execute specific movements to show the form of a piece of music.

♪ They can create their own instruments using a Makey Makey kit.

G Suite for Education

This section will focus on the various Google tools that can empower music students in your classroom. For schools that do not use G Suite for Education, Office365 offers some similar applications.

Google Classroom

Google Classroom is a virtual classroom space that can streamline workflow, manage assignments, and connect with students. Tools such as Flipgrid, Noteflight, Soundtrap, and more can now integrate with Google Classroom, allowing increased functionality for music teachers. With Google Classroom, teachers can easily distribute and collect assignments, as well as leave feedback for students.

Here are some suggestions for using Google Classroom to empower music students:

♪ Assign a playing test where students submit videos of themselves performing a specific skill, giving them a choice in how to demonstrate mastery of that skill.

♪ Distribute a form where they can vote for their favorite pieces, giving them a choice in performance repertoire.

♪ Distribute and collect reflection and goal-setting documents, giving students a voice in their learning path.

♪ Using the discussion features, engage students in digital conversation to spark connections within the class.

♪ Curate video tutorials and/or additional songs so students can take ownership by getting extra help when needed or extending their learning beyond what's covered in class.

Google Slides

Google Slides is so versatile! Many people think of it as a presentation tool, which it is quite successfully; creating a presentation in slides is easy enough for students of most ages to handle. But you can also use Google Slides collaboratively, with multiple students or even an entire class working on one slide deck together.

To do this, first create the slide deck and share it (maybe via Google Classroom) so everyone can edit the document. Use the first slide for instructions and any information your students should have prior to beginning their work. Instruct them to add a new slide and then answer or create something to match a prompt. Alternatively, instead of having them create a new slide, you could duplicate a slide enough times to have one ready for each student. The benefit of sharing one slide deck with an entire class is that all students can view and comment on one another's work. This can even connect multiple sections of a class where students rarely get to work together.

Here are some ideas for using Google Slides to empower music students:

> ♪ Using a collaborative slide deck, have each student reflect on a recent performance, sharing his or her voice. Then ask the students to read and comment on two additional students' responses.

> ♪ Using a collaborative slide deck, have each student create a slide documenting their favorite memory from a recent performance, trip, or the school year. Play the slide show at the beginning of a performance or awards night, showcasing each student's voice and creation.

> ♪ Have each student create their own slide deck and use it as a digital portfolio throughout the school year. They can add videos, pictures, and reflections to the slides, creating a digital representation of their accomplishments.

> ♪ Create a collaborative slide deck where students can ask questions related to a new piece of music, another piece of music they've listened to, a performance they attended, or something else. Encourage them to return to the slide deck to add answers they've found or additional questions.

> ♪ Create a collaborative slide deck to curate a collection of original rhythmic patterns and activities for students' peers using Noteflight or the Flat for Docs add-on.

Flat for Docs

Flat for Docs is an add-on that allows the user to enter music notation directly into Google Slides and Google Docs. This has a whole range of potential uses for music teachers, and it can easily be used by music students as well. Once you've added Flat to your Google Slides or Docs add-on menu, it will be available every time you open the application. Students can use the Flat add-on to compose original melodies or complete digital dictation tasks. Flat even has a playback feature, so they can hear what their compositions sound like within the add-on! Have them compose using paper and pencil first, then they can input their compositions into Flat as a bonus. Flat is also available as stand-alone online music notation software, containing numerous collaborative and integrative features. For more information, visit www.flat.io.

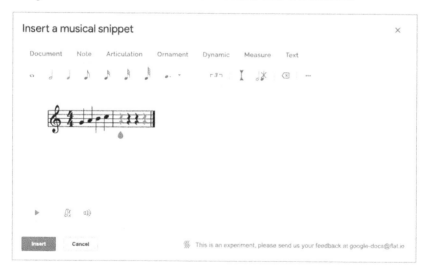

Flat for Docs

Google Meet

Google Meet allows you to chat and make video calls. Video calls can be very beneficial in music classes to connect students to composers, conductors, performers, other educators and classrooms, and more. In the past, for a connection like this to be successful, you'd need to find someone in your city or at least within driving distance. Google Meet removes that limitation completely. As long as you can make the timing work, you can connect with anyone in the world! Consider some of these ideas to empower students by connecting them using Google Meet:

> ♪ Connect with a composer whose piece you are playing, either to clinic the piece or have a question-and-answer session.
>
> ♪ Connect with a professional to give a masterclass on their instrument.
>
> ♪ Connect with another class or ensemble to perform for each other before a concert, assessment, or festival.

Chrome Music Lab and Other Chrome Experiments

The Chrome Music Lab is one of Google's many experiments that can lead you down a rabbit hole if you're not careful! The Chrome Music Lab contains several tools you can use to create and experiment with music. There are tools for creating songs, melodies, and rhythms, as well as tools to connect musical elements to science, math, and art. Using the Chrome Music Lab requires no formal music training, so students of all ages can use and appreciate these tools.

> ♪ Students can use the Song Maker or Melody Maker to create their own music.
>
> ♪ After creating something in the Song Maker, they can save their songs and share them via a link provided, allowing them to share their musical voices.
>
> ♪ They can use the Rhythm tool to have a choice in creating a background track for a song, activity, or exercise.
>
> ♪ They can use Sound Waves, Harmonics, or the Voice Spinner to experiment and ask questions about how various manipulations impact sound.

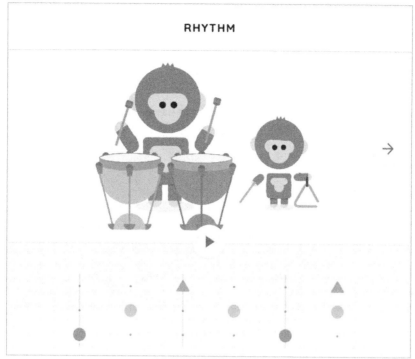

Chrome Music Lab: Rhythm

Another Chrome Experiment worth mentioning is the Semi-Conductor, which uses AI technology and the camera on your device to allow you to conduct an orchestra! The orchestra responds to your movement, adjusting tempo, volume, and even instrumentation.[2] Students will love creating and making musical choices in this way.

The Seeing Music tool creates a visual representation of sounds it hears, coming from either a voice, an instrument, an audio upload, or prerecorded options.[3] Many vocal music teachers will use this tool along with vocal warm-ups, projecting it on the board so students can "see" what they are singing. By having one student at a time serve as the leader, or model, for these warm-ups, you're providing a great opportunity for each of them to share their musical voice.

Groove Pizza is similar to the Rhythm tool in the Chrome Music Lab, but has several additional features. Students create rhythms by adding to different layers of the pizza. The tempo, volume, subdivisions, and instruments are all adjustable.[4] Students can develop their own grooves to accompany a song or rap, or even experiment with how different choices impact the overall sound. Groove Pizza also allows you to add a STEAM component by exploring the various shapes and angles created within the pizza.

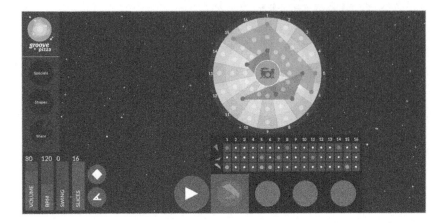

Groove Pizza

Flipgrid

Flipgrid has been mentioned before in this book, and it's worth bringing up again. Flipgrid is a video-based social-learning program perfect for amplifying student voice. Teachers set up a "grid," which is basically their virtual classroom. Within the grid, they create topics, which are the specific assignments or prompts that students create video responses for. When students are done with their response, the video shows up in the grid. They can watch all the videos in the grid and leave video replies for their classmates.

Flipgrid is a great tool for empowering music students since it touches on almost every quality you're seeking to develop in them. Students are creating videos and sharing their voices, both musical and spoken. They can share videos not only within their classes but also with other classes around the world, professionals, families, and community members! Since all sharing occurs within the grid, it's a safe way for them to connect with others. Flipgrid also encourages them to take ownership of their learning. We've seen students, after being inspired by watching other kids share their music, take it upon themselves to learn new things and seek further instructions.

Recently a colleague, Brittany Gonzalez, used Flipgrid to have her students communicate with an artist in residence, Baba Bomani. He had visited the school several times, working with students on creating their own personal raps. The project combined the writing process with hip-hop music, and they loved it! Following the experience, Brittany had the students create thank-you videos for Baba using the same process. She could have easily had them write thank-you notes, but this way they could use the skills they learned from the artist and share them with him directly.

Here are a few ways to use Flipgrid to empower music students in your classrooms:

♪ Students can create videos as a formative assessment demonstrating specific skills, often having a choice in what songs to play.

♪ They can create reflection videos following a performance, event, or semester.

♪ They can create "almost ready" videos before solo or ensemble performances, then provide video feedback for themselves and classmates.

♪ They can use Flipgrid as a digital portfolio, curating videos that demonstrate their learning throughout the school year and adding reflections with each video.

♪ You can connect two or more classrooms on one grid, having students share videos for a specific purpose.

Digital Learning Portfolios

Portfolios have existed in English classes, art studios, and the workplace for years. People collect samples of their work in one place to show growth, skills, and accomplishments. Now it's easier than ever to do this in music too! Almost everyone has access to a video camera or recording device, which enables students to create their own digital portfolios.

We should include a quick shout-out to Pat Bove, a phenomenal retired elementary-music teacher from Pennsylvania who used to do this with cassette tapes. She would have parent volunteers come in two or three times each year and record individual students singing. By the time they graduated from fifth grade, each student had a cassette tape documenting their vocal progress over the years. If Pat only knew how easy this would eventually become!

Digital portfolios can serve several purposes. They can form a curated collection, acting as a showcase of a student's musical accomplishments, eventually to be published or shared otherwise with a larger audience. They can also document the learning process, showing how a student grows musically over time. In a process-driven portfolio, students reflect on their performance, receive feedback, and make changes as needed.

Hybrid portfolios contain the best of both worlds. Students collect music samples, reflect, receive feedback, make changes, and then publish.[5] When you are thinking about empowering your students, it's important that they have a voice in what goes into their portfolio. They can include any number of artifacts, such as musical compositions, technology projects, research-based projects, performances, and more. They should reflect on their work, regardless of whether the reflection goes in the actual portfolio. With a digital platform, there are very few limits to what is possible. Allow students to personalize the experience. The more they can be directly involved in the curation process, the better.

The technology options for a digital portfolio are numerous. If your school uses G Suite for Education, consider using one of the Google tools to host the portfolios. Google Sites are perfect for this, though Google Slides and even Google Drive will also work. Many teachers, music and otherwise, use Seesaw in their classrooms. Seesaw also provides opportunities to create digital portfolios. ClassDojo used to be a platform only for classroom management, but it has expanded to include portfolio features. YouTube and Vimeo might also work, for older students. There are countless other tools available; you just need to find the tool that is right for you, your students, and your available technology.

When choosing a tool for a musical digital portfolio, think about your end goal. Is this something you want students to work on for a school year or for their entire school career?

What technology do they have access to? Computers? Chromebooks? Tablets? Each has its own benefits and limitations you will need to explore before proceeding. Also think about who will have access to the digital portfolio. Will students be able to share it with future schools or employers? At the same time, is student privacy being maintained? With careful research and a conversation with your school technology coach, you'll be able to find a tool that suits the needs of your music students.

Coda

While this chapter could never include all the available tech tools for student empowerment, we hope that it has provided ideas. Hopefully, you also see that even nonmusic tools can work. Not every tool will work with every classroom, but we're confident you can find something that will work for you. Always refer back to your goal. What do you want your students to learn? How can you give them ownership within that process? What tech tool can maximize your efforts?

It's important to say that sometimes technology won't be the right fit. Please don't add tech tools because you think you have to. Add them with purpose. After you use a tech tool, reflect on the student and teacher experience. Did the students accomplish the learning goals? Was the technology an aide in the process or a hindrance? Did the process take too long or was the technology efficient? All these questions are important factors to consider for future lessons. If the whole process didn't work, throw it out and start again. If there were great parts that worked but a few glitches, work to improve the glitches so that the next lesson can be even better. Trying new things is always a learning process, and you rarely hit a home run on the first try. It takes time to find the right integration and balance.

Things to Try Tomorrow

♪ Using a DAW, have students create a rhythmic backing track for a song they are learning. Experiment with different tempos and styles.

♪ Have them create a short melody in the Chrome Music Lab's Song Maker, showing ascending and descending melodic lines.

♪ Use Flipgrid for students to share their goals for an upcoming performance or unit of study.

Continue the conversation: share what you tried with #PasstheBatonBook!

Encore: Blended Learning with Ashley Cuthbertson

Ashley Cuthbertson, an elementary general and vocal music teacher in Northern Virginia, creates blended playlists to empower students learning to play the recorder. In her school, third-grade students learn to play the recorder starting in January. Instead of using direct instruction each week, having students move through the recorder curriculum together, Ashley uses the playlists so they can work at their own pace and set goals appropriate to their skill level and learning style.

Class begins with Ashley teaching a mini lesson that includes a warm-up and an introduction to any new material, such as pitches, melodic patterns, or rhythms. Students then access the playlist in Google Classroom and work through the content individually. The playlist is divided into lessons, with each incorporating a specific learning target, such as playing melodic patterns on the recorder using three notes. The playlists look similar to what you might see on YouTube, but they're housed in Google Classroom, so students have access to video tutorials created by Ashley, PowerPoint links, and any other digital content that might support them in mastering the learning target.

She offers this variety of learning materials so students can choose those that help them learn the best. At the end of each lesson, they must submit a video assessment in Flipgrid demonstrating their learning. Since they're working at their own pace, they can reread or rewatch the content as many times as needed. This would not be possible if Ashley were delivering all of the content in person, to everyone at the same time.

To make the playlist model successful, she had to shift her instruction to maximize the time students work on their own and minimize the time she was directly instructing the class. By focusing on the mini lesson as the foundation of the class, she could then work with small groups who needed more guided instruction and offer personalized feedback on the formative assessments that were turned in after each lesson.

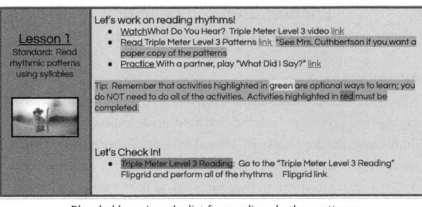

Blended learning playlist for reading rhythm patterns

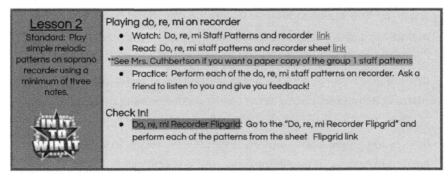

Blended learning playlist for playing simple melodic patterns

Ashley has found this model to be extremely engaging for the students. They're excited and motivated to work hard. They like being able to move ahead in the playlist when they've mastered the content, and they appreciate having choices in the process. Because they develop the skills on their own (after the mini lesson), they have a deeper understanding of the patterns and songs.

Prior to using playlists for recorder instruction, Ashley used many of the tech tools to support other areas of her music curriculum. Students were already familiar with the G Suite for Education tools and Flipgrid, having used them both in music and general education classrooms. If someone is interested in trying blended learning playlists with their music students, Ashley recommends scaffolding to meet the needs of the students. Since hers were accustomed to using the tech tools, she could dive right into the playlists without much difficulty. Building upon the skills and tools students already have will increase your chances of success.

Connect with Ashley!

♪ email: a.cuthbertson14@gmail.com
♪ Twitter: @ACuthbertson10

12

The Empowered Music Teacher

*Change is the opportunity to
do something amazing.*
—George Couros

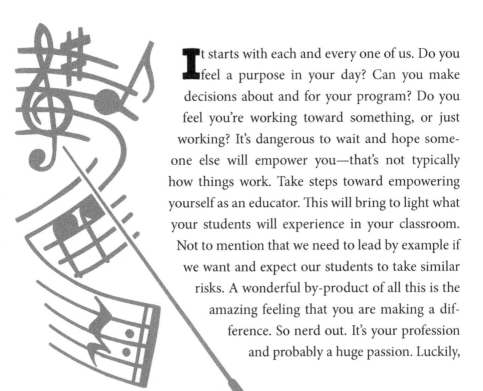

It starts with each and every one of us. Do you feel a purpose in your day? Can you make decisions about and for your program? Do you feel you're working toward something, or just working? It's dangerous to wait and hope someone else will empower you—that's not typically how things work. Take steps toward empowering yourself as an educator. This will bring to light what your students will experience in your classroom. Not to mention that we need to lead by example if we want and expect our students to take similar risks. A wonderful by-product of all this is the amazing feeling that you are making a difference. So nerd out. It's your profession and probably a huge passion. Luckily, just by reading this book, you've put yourself on the path to becoming an empowered music teacher.

Daniel Pink's research about autonomy, mastery, and purpose extends beyond our students to our own lives as well. When thinking about autonomy, don't assume that means you're in this alone. He says, "Autonomy, as they see it, is different from independence. It's not the rugged, go-it-alone, rely-on-nobody individualism of the American cowboy. It means acting with choice—which means we can be both autonomous and happily interdependent with others." Autonomy is the freedom to tailor professional development to your own needs. It's the motivation to set goals for yourself and work little by little to achieve them. It's the ability to make decisions for yourself as an educator and as a musician.

Many times throughout this book, we've asked you to think about your goals for your students, as that will drive your decisions moving forward. Those goals provide a purpose for what you do. Now we'll also encourage you to think about your own goals, and your own purpose. To truly find motivation in your work and to move toward being an empowered educator, you must have a purpose. This can come in many forms. When we struggle with an ensemble or with meeting the needs of a few individuals in our classroom, we have a reason to learn new strategies to best serve those students. When we discover that our repertoire primarily represents one culture, we have a purpose for researching more diverse musicians.

Striving to achieve mastery requires having the self-discipline to work daily toward learning something new or achieving a specific skill. Whether it involves practicing a rehearsal technique, reflecting on your instruction, learning new tech tools for the classroom, or even sharpening your piano accompaniment skills, mastery in some area should always be a goal. In our profession, there's never a dull moment. We're constantly adjusting our instruction to meet the needs of all students. It's what makes our jobs so challenging and yet so rewarding. Our constant effort to improve and work toward mastery drives many of us as educators.

George Couros, the author of *The Innovator's Mindset*, reminds us, "Often the biggest barrier to innovation is our own way of thinking." We challenge you to stop focusing on what you can't do and instead put energy into the small shifts you can make.

You Have a Voice

Reading is like breathing in, writing is like breathing out.
—Pam Allyn

Do you share your voice? Do you speak up to advocate for your program and your students? Do you share things that you're doing and that your students are doing? Think of ways you can share your own voice and ensure that it is heard. This could be anything from an email blast to your faculty sharing the accomplishments of your students at a festival to presenting a workshop in your district or at a professional conference. You have a voice, and others need to hear it.

> **Theresa:** I initially found my voice through blogging. What started as a guest post for EdTechTeam turned into creating my own blog and posting two to three times each month. Not only do I enjoy sharing my voice in this way, I also value the reflective process I go through when crafting each post. Each lesson or activity I write about causes me to stop and think: *What was my goal for my students? Did they accomplish it? What purpose did this activity serve? What would I do differently next time?* While some may be content with writing this in a personal journal or diary, for me, preparing each post for an audience made it that much more meaningful.

When you truly use your voice as an empowered music teacher, you determine both what and how you will learn. All teachers can begin by taking time to reflect on their practice and on setting goals for themselves. Some school systems have even embedded this into the teacher evaluation system. Reflection and goal setting in this situation can sometimes feel contrived or forced, so find an authentic means that works for you. Even if it's just spending three minutes jotting down thoughts on a Post-it Note after a lesson or rehearsal, making this practice a habit will benefit you and your students.

What are your goals as an educator? This doesn't mean your goals for your students; what are your goals for *you*? Do you want to talk less during rehearsals? Become a more confident piano player? Create better transitions between activities in a class? Set a goal and come up with a plan for meeting it.

Kathryn: After reading *Shift This!* by Joy Kirr, I was encouraged to create a mission statement for myself and my school year. I set three goals and spent time typing, printing, and laminating it to display near my desk. The first year I tried this, I was surprised at how well it pushed my thinking. Near the end of the year, I looked at the goals and reflected on my growth. I was amazed by the power of committing the words to print and posting them where I could see them daily. Just by putting the goals out there, I was able to focus my efforts on what was most important.

AS AN ELEMENTARY GENERAL
MUSIC TEACHER I WILL:

...CELEBRATE THE CREATIVE
SIDE OF ALL KIDS AND
ENCOURAGE GROWTH

...MODEL RISK TAKING AND
SHARE FAILURES WITH MY
STUDENTS

...TAKE TIME FOR EMPATHY-
BUILDING CONVERSATIONS
BECAUSE HELPING KIDS BE
THEIR BEST SELF MATTERS

...FIND MORE WAYS TO ALLOW
CHILDREN CHOICE AND VOICE
IN THEIR LEARNING

...FOSTER A ROOM THAT
ENGAGES ALL IN SONG AND
PLAY

PIC·COLLAGE

Kathryn's mission statement

You Have Choices

You deserve to have a say in choosing your path, whatever that may be. Take charge of your professional learning. Seek opportunities and resources that will help you grow as an educator. For both of us, attending our state music educator conference is a highlight each year. We also highly recommend finding an Edcamp in your area. Edcamps are not music specific, but they draw many educators who want to make a difference, learn new ideas, and improve their craft. An Edcamp is considered an "unconference," in that there is no preset schedule; everything is attendee driven. In addition, attendees follow the "rule of two feet"—if a session or topic doesn't resonate with you, you are encouraged to use your two feet to find one that does! We learn something new at each Edcamp we attend, and the time spent with like-minded educators is valuable. Are you interested in finding or starting an Edcamp in your area? Check out www.edcamp.org.

We have no choice about many aspects of our workdays. We must arrive at a specified time, teach specified classes, eat lunch when told . . . the list goes on. It's important to find some places where you do have choices and take advantage of them. Are you given a choice of professional development sessions to attend? Do you have flexibility in committees to join or projects to work on within the school system? You make decisions about your classroom every day, so you should make them for yourself as well. You also determine your attitude toward the areas of work where you don't have a choice. You can make them something big, or something not so big. When we choose not to let something small bother us, the rest of the day is typically much more enjoyable. Keeping positivity in the workplace is important for your mindset and your work with students.

Ask Questions

*When teachers undertake research, they deepen and
improve their teaching relationships with children
and with one another as professionals.*
—Barbara Henderson, Daniel R. Meier, and Gail Perry

When was the last time you let yourself dive deep after something you were curious about? And we're not referring to mindless scrolling through social media. When have you done actual research? Or when have you questioned something you have always done or your organization has always done? Do you ever ask, "Is there value in doing this still?"

Often when we ask questions, we want to find an immediate answer. Our world is full of instant gratification, as we can answer most questions with a simple Google search. Instead, spend time with your question. Bring it up at a team meeting or with a trusted friend to get the ball rolling. Attend a workshop or Edcamp, keeping your eyes and ears open to any content that might be helpful to your research. Give yourself permission to ask questions, dig deep, and find answers. If you're asking questions of yourself, such as why a specific rule or regulation exists in your classroom, consider the technique "Five Whys." Ask and answer the question "Why?" five times in a row to get to the heart of the matter. Once there, decide if whatever is in question is really what's best for your classroom and your students.

You can take these questions to the next level by engaging in teacher research. According to Diane DeMott Painter, former coleader of the Fairfax County Teacher Research Network, "Teacher research is practical, action-based research. It enables educators to follow their interests and their needs as they investigate what they and their students do. Teachers who practice teacher research find that it expands and enriches their teaching skills and puts them in collaborative contact with peers that have a like interest in classroom research."[1]

When you take time to conduct research, you do more than ask questions. You collect data, analyze results, and share your findings. Throughout the process, you learn about yourself, your students, and your teaching. You gain information that can benefit all three areas.

NAfME includes research as one pillar of its 2016–2021 Strategic Plan. It's their goal to use research "to promote and disseminate sound data to advance music teaching and learning and influence educational policy."[2] NAfME, along with the Society for Research in Music Education (SRME), accepts proposals for their Biennial Music Research and Teacher Education Conference, as well as research grants for projects relating to important issues in music education.[3]

Teacher research is something you can engage in alone or with a group of trusted friends. Theresa recently joined a Teacher Research Club within her school district. The group comprises teachers who want to learn more about various topics important to them. They meet monthly to discuss their progress and will share their findings at the end of the school year with a celebration.

Your questions don't have to be formal or involved, but taking the time to ask and find answers empowers you as an educator, benefitting you and your students.

You Are a Creator

We became music educators because of a love and passion for making music. There was a time in our lives when performing and practicing our instruments was the primary focus. Many of us can remember spending hours every day in college locked in a practice room. Aside from attending rehearsals, that was the most important part of the week! Fast-forward to when we entered the workforce, and for many of us the practice room became a distant memory. Lesson plans, concert prep, and report-card grades took over. Some weeks we never even touch our instruments. If this is your current experience, we challenge you to dust off your instrument and create music. Sit in with a community ensemble, work up a solo piece to perform for your students, jam with some friends, or just practice for the sake of practicing! You might surprise yourself with how good it feels.

If performing isn't your cup of tea, think about another way you could create. Music composition? Art? Writing? It may come as no surprise that we found writing an amazing source for creating. Other music-teacher friends enjoy crochet, photography, painting, and cooking. Find a creative outlet. It will no doubt strengthen you as a musician and an educator.

Whatever you do, please don't say you aren't creative. You are. We all are. We create lessons daily. We create a safe environment and various experiences for our students. We do ourselves a huge disservice when we say we aren't creative. Find your passions and strengths, then share and get feedback. We learn so much more about ourselves and our own learning by doing so. When we share our creations with the world, we give to others and get so much back in return.

Whatever you do, please don't say you aren't creative. You are.

You Are Connected

There are many passionate educators online ready to share and grow their craft. A PLN (professional learning network) is an invaluable (and free!) virtual resource we highly suggest looking into, if you haven't already. Many educators find great value in developing a PLN on social media.

Kathryn: I met Theresa through Twitter while participating in a MOOC (massive open online course) in 2017. The course consisted of watching YouTube Live sessions from amazing educators, reading a book, and blogging weekly. Twitter chats were encouraged as well to keep the conversation going. She and I connected during one of the first Twitter chats. We began to follow each other's blog, and we have pushed each other's thinking ever since. We follow our respective classroom social media pages, have connected our classrooms on several occasions, presented together at the International Music Education Summit, appeared on the *Music Ed Mentor* podcast, and we talk multiple times a day.

Theresa: At first, I couldn't understand why my school district was encouraging teachers to set up Twitter accounts. Teachers on social media? Sharing about students? There seemed like so many things wrong with that concept. But I obliged and set up my account. For the first six months I posted occasionally, when it was convenient. I followed several other teachers in my area and some music teachers who were easy to find, and that was it—until I took a professional development course and was encouraged to participate in a Twitter chat. That was my lightbulb moment. I discovered through hashtags how to find people who had similar interests. And I learned that Twitter wasn't just about me posting things happening in my classroom, it was seeing what other people did in theirs and having conversations about it. When I follow other teachers, I can learn from what they do. And when I share things, others can learn from me. It's an amazing concept that I still value.

Our PLN consists of educators, administrators, speakers, authors, composers, conductors, and more. These are people who want the same things we do: to grow as humans and to help others do the same. It doesn't matter if you choose Twitter, Facebook, Instagram, or the newest social media platform, as long as you find it and use it. It's okay to be critical about who you let into your PLN. If someone is a negative influence, don't feel obligated to follow and engage with them! This is for you and your growth. At the same time, find people who are good at areas you want to improve in. Learn from them.

"Starting a journey on a social media platform can be life changing." We've heard people say this so many times at conferences and in conversation, and yet no one can articulate why. It's hard to explain, partly because you really don't know what will happen until you join and start a conversation.

We would not have believed anyone who said we'd meet someone online and write a book with them, but that is our story. We can live eleven hours away from each other and collaborate on multiple projects with ease. Joining social media has transformed our careers in ways we could have never imagined. So our best advice is to start your journey and see where it takes you!

If social media still isn't your thing, or if you'd rather keep Facebook for family and friends, there are other ways to connect with teachers outside of your building and district. You can always attend events such as your state Music Educators Association conference, or the annual NAfME conference. Many other organizations, such as OAKE, AOSA, ASTA, and ACDA, also hold yearly conferences. While conferences are great for the sessions you can attend, the networking is just as valuable! Start conversations. We often think of experts in our field as people who present, write books, and have a large online presence, forgetting the teacher in a nearby district with years of experience, or someone across the country with a blog. We have so much we can offer one another; we live in the trenches daily! Don't discount the educators in your district or in your network. They are a great resource.

Own Your Process

Life begins at the end of your comfort zone.
—Neale Donald Walsch

*You can't expect your students to learn
every day if you don't.*
—Adam Welcome

When you are using your voice, making choices, creating, connecting, and asking questions, you are truly owning your process. This is the goal for any empowered music teacher *or* student.

We've said it before and we'll say it again: Take ownership of your professional development. Expand your learning beyond your specific teaching position because you can gain so much from a different lens or perspective. As an instrumental music teacher, Theresa has gained a lot from the general and vocal music workshops she's attended. She loves learning about how the students are taught in general music, prior to starting in band. It gives her great insight into where to begin, so she isn't reinventing the wheel.

We also listen to podcasts relating to entrepreneurship, marketing, social media, and writing. While the writing podcasts may seem obvious choices (we did finally manage to finish this book!), the others made sense too. As music teachers, we must constantly advocate for our programs—or, in other words, sell others on what we do. Who better to learn from than entrepreneurs and marketing professionals? And honestly, those topics interest us. They don't directly relate to teaching music, but that's okay. They help us to grow as people and therefore as educators as well.

School-mandated professional development may or may not relate to you, but try to find some value in it regardless. Go in with an open mind. Even if you only gain a better understanding of what colleagues are dealing with, that can help you in future interactions. Also, ask your administration for personalized professional development for your music department. Often administrators struggle to know what to offer music educators, and they will welcome suggestions. You never know until you ask.

When you're ready, lead a professional development session yourself. You learn so much when you take on that role. Share your passion, process, and what you have learned. It's okay to admit you aren't an expert; it's still valuable for others to hear about your experience—the successes *and* the failures. We are all learning together.

Consider taking part in or creating your own book study. Choose a book that is mutually interesting to you and others, set up a reading schedule, and discuss the book with other readers in person or virtually. A virtual book study is a great way to connect with other music educators, maybe even members of your newly formed PLN. We've participated in several online book studies, on a variety of platforms: through Facebook groups and Twitter chats, using Padlet, Google Docs, and even Voxer. The platform doesn't matter. What matters is the commitment of the participants.

Owning the process will look different for everyone. Doug Conrad, a band director in Pennsylvania, created the *Directors Circle* podcast. He enjoyed listening to podcasts about music education but felt there needed to be more material related to leadership in the field. His podcast allows him to share his voice, connect with inspiring music educators, and create a resource for other teachers. Theresa Turner, an elementary music teacher in Texas, took learning into her own hands by creating a Twitter chat using the hashtag #elmusedchat. Theresa saw value in the chats she was participating in but noticed a lack of content specifically for elementary music teachers. Her chat occurs weekly, engaging music teachers from a variety of backgrounds and locations.

Both Doug Conrad and Theresa Turner took learning into their own hands. They didn't wait for someone else to come along and create what they felt was missing; they did it themselves. That's what an empowered educator looks like.

Coda

If you want to go fast, go alone.
If you want to go far, go together.

Empowering your students begins with empowering yourself as a musician and as an educator. Please do not only consume this information. Read it, understand it, and make a change!

♪ Use your voice and make choices for yourself and your students.

♪ Get in touch with your inner musician. Create something that makes you happy.

♪ Connect with others. Think about who can help you reach your goals and who you can help along the way.

♪ Ask questions. Give yourself permission to dive into the rabbit hole to find the answers.

♪ Take ownership. Learn something new, explore a passion. You deserve it.

And remember to take care of yourself. Rest, reset, and recharge. Sometimes owning the process means you have to take a step back and look at the big picture. A music teacher running on empty will not help anyone. Don't do everything yourself. As humans, we need a community around us. Use your friends, coworkers, and your PLN. We are not alone in this journey.

Things to Try Tomorrow

♪ If you haven't found your PLN, create it! Use Twitter, Facebook, Instagram, or whatever the newest platform is and find your people. Consider following #PasstheBatonBook, #musedchat, #elmusedchat, #EmpowerBook, #ShiftThis, #BlairFinchProject, #TLAP, #InnovatorsMindset, and #LearnLAP.

♪ Start a blog, vlog, or journal for yourself, to document this journey. What works, what doesn't, and what are you most excited about?

♪ Connect with other music-teacher friends to start a book club, either in person or virtually.

♪ Reconnect with your inner musician. Spend some time with your instrument, composing or even just listening to music that makes you happy.

♪ Take a few minutes to think about your goals—as a music educator, musician, and person. What is the first step needed toward one of those goals? That first step is often the most important. Take it!

Continue the conversation: share what you tried with #PasstheBatonBook!

13

Final Thoughts

You've made it this far with us, and hopefully you're excited about the prospects ahead. We imagine there are still some questions, hesitations, and concerns, which we'll try to clarify here. In the classroom, you might think you don't have time for one more thing—but rather than looking at it like that, picture instead a shift in what you are currently doing. You're already teaching your students to be good musicians; now you'll do so with the intention of student ownership.

What About the Curriculum/Standards?

Remember, the National Core Art Standards should be at the forefront of what we do, and they drive our curriculum. The standards require that students are creating, performing, connecting, and responding. They enable meaningful reflection, contain verbiage for assessments, and focus on music appreciation as well as music literacy. These standards are written from the viewpoint of the student's experience and not the educator's. Therefore, when we unpack the standards, we should look for the action words (such as analyze, evaluate, and refine) describing student learning under the four categories: Creating, Performing, Connecting, and Responding. The National Core Art Standards are a great guide in helping music educators empower their students.

Empowered students take responsibility for the planning, creating, refining, and presenting of their musical product. By working within the curriculum to engage in a creation project, they get time to grapple with an essential question and practice specific musical skills. When they explore and research a passion related to music but personalized to their own interests, they can respond and connect to the music around them. They can select repertoire for performance and evaluation, and they are encouraged to connect this music to their personal experiences and daily lives. We don't have to abandon the curriculum; we're simply making adjustments to how it's implemented.

Tackling Traditions

The most dangerous phrase . . .
is "We've always done it that way."
—Rear Admiral Grace Hopper

While you were reading this book, there may have been times you paused to reflect on something you do in your current teaching practice. In fact, we hope this is the case! It's possible you've found aspects of your music-teaching practice that are not empowering to students, but with a few small tweaks could be. So many of us continue to do the same things over and over simply because that's the way we've always done it, or because our community demands it. But the empowered music teacher needs to take a deeper look. In striving to empower our music students, we must ask ourselves, "Why?"

This is especially true in music education, a field deeply rooted in tradition. There will be times when you look at a traditional approach to something and ask yourself why it's being done that way. Only because it's a tradition? Or because there's musical and educational value in it? If there is no such value, it may be time to make some changes.

A great example of this is the shift away from traditional performances for younger students. Many music teachers feel that formal performances focus too much on a final product and take away from valuable time to work on the music curriculum. Instead of completely eliminating this traditional performance, teachers have shifted to informance events, which focus more on the music-making process. The students are still "performing," but in a much more educational and informal way. Of course, we suggest music educators take this process further to encourage the student's voice and choice. Give them ownership of the process. Plan with them and let them choose what learning they wish to share with the audience.

We're not suggesting you throw all traditions out the window; only that you reevaluate. It's always important to look at the values of the school and your music program. Think back, again, to the goals you set in Chapter 1. How can you make a small adjustment to the tradition in question to better align with your values and goals? How can you give your students a more empowering role? Sometimes you'll find that keeping a highly valued tradition is necessary, and that's fine too. At least take the time to ask questions and examine your choices.

Start Small, but Don't Skip Steps

Regardless of where you are on the empowerment spectrum, whether your classes are completely teacher directed or if you've started to empower your students, remember to take baby steps. It's through small, intentional shifts that you will make a difference. One thing to be cautious of: *Do not rush through or skip steps in the process!* Attempting to rush and give students too much freedom right away can be detrimental to the desired outcome. When that happens, because it happens to all of us, take a step back, reflect, and try again.

Students who have never been asked their thoughts or opinions before may be hesitant to speak up, or may have very "shallow" responses in the beginning. Try having them share their thoughts with a friend or neighbor first, before sharing with the entire class. When you're giving them choices, have them pick from two or three familiar options first. When they're creating, ensure that they have the tools and background knowledge necessary to complete the task. If you're asking young musicians to analyze a piece of music, make sure they understand and can apply those analytical skills first.

The same applies to you, the teacher. Give yourself permission to start small. Rushing to a perceived "finish line" will only cause anxiety, and you risk quitting before you even begin. Pick one thing you can do tomorrow. See how that goes, adjust as needed, and when you're ready, take the next step.

It's Going to Be Messy

Embrace letting go. When students are empowered, they no longer rely on the teacher for all music-making opportunities. They will make it happen on their  own. As a result, there will be times when they are scattered around the room, working on different projects, playing at different times. This is okay. While from the outside it may look, and even sound, like chaos, upon closer examination you will see music-making in progress.

> **Kathryn:** I've noticed I can handle what may look like chaos so much better than a few years ago. I can better anticipate what my students might need and where they will struggle. Each year, the chaos diminishes, and they can do more. As I gain experience, I'm more comfortable with students going different directions, and I'm better at supporting and guiding them. Do your best and embrace the trial and error.

Are you worried about what an administrator or colleague might say when walking by on a particularly noisy day? Beat them to the punch. Share with others your goals and your plans for achieving them. Then, when ready, invite administrators and colleagues into your class to see what your students are doing. Point out the collaboration, creativity, and ownership that is taking place. Be open to feedback yourself as you're on this journey. Remember that you don't have to be perfect before trying something new. In fact, you most likely will never try it if you wait until you're ready! Be vulnerable. Isn't that what you're asking from your students?

Classroom Management

We just told you that a classroom with empowered students will seem messy and noisy at times, and that is accurate. However, for students to be successful, there must be some order within the new environment. Establishing systems, routines, and expectations is necessary for productivity in any music classroom.

When creating expectations, keep it simple. Determine three to five things everyone must do in the music room. When you frame expectations positively you're agreeing upon what your students will do, as opposed to what they won't. Ideally, you can work together to determine the expectations for the class. By doing this, students immediately take ownership in the classroom.

Theresa: One system I used in my elementary instrumental-music classroom helped my students when practicing independently during group lessons. They would spread out around the room to work on skills of their choice while I circulated around the room, checking in and helping as needed. Often they would have questions or problems but find themselves waiting in line for me to finish helping another student. To make this more efficient, they used the clothespin system. I gave each student a bag with three clothespins: green, yellow, and red. They were to have one clothespin clipped to the top of their music stand at all times. The green clothespin symbolized they were fine and didn't need any help. The yellow clothespin meant the student had a question or a problem, but it wasn't urgent, or might be something a classmate could help with. They were instructed to keep practicing when the yellow clip was up and to move on to something different if needed. The red clothespin meant there was an urgent problem, such as an instrument falling apart.

The clothespin system required students to think through their question or problem to determine how urgent it was. Most times they would change the clip to yellow, only to figure out the answer independently and return it to green before help even arrived. It also gave them the opportunity to take ownership and help a friend when they were able to. While clothespins worked best on the music stands, I've seen other teachers do similar things with colored plastic cups.

Part of this process is taking the time to teach skills your students lack. They don't always know how to practice effectively and efficiently, and may not understand what a good practice space looks and feels like. They don't always have the organizational skills to remember when their lesson is and how to get their instruments and materials to and from school. Some struggle within ensemble rehearsals or general music lessons. They don't always advocate when they don't understand a concept, or when they struggle with attention deficits, making it harder to concentrate on the learning tasks. The upside to an empowered classroom is that students are given the opportunity to lead, understand themselves as learners and musicians, and own the process successfully.

Kathryn: I can predict ways my students might struggle when working in a small group. To help prepare them for this, I review a few strategies to use if a conflict occurs. Paul Solarz, author of *Learn Like a Pirate*, has three great suggestions for conflict resolution, and they work well in the general music classroom. His three strategies are (1) Rock-Paper-Scissors, (2) Compromise, and (3) Choose Kind. If there's an argument, ask your students if they could resolve it over a game of Rock-Paper-Scissors. Other times, we can take both ideas and compromise. And there is always value in choosing kind. I'm amazed at how many will choose this and let go of their good idea in favor of a classmate's. It's a great chance to help your students see and reinforce human kindness. So, before I send mine off into small groups, I ask them what strategies they can use when a conflict arises, and I challenge them to be the leader in the group and offer a suggestion when that happens.

Like Theresa's clothespin system, this leaves me available to walk around the room and check in with my students. There may be a group I need to supervise more closely or confer with when the outcome isn't meeting expectations. This is natural during the learning process. When you offer leadership opportunities and step out of the way whenever possible, students can take more control of the learning.

Reexamine the Space

As you embrace this new classroom dynamic, it may be time to reexamine your learning space. What experiences and opportunities do you want your students to have? Does your space allow for these to occur? In Theresa's instrumental classroom, the space needed to work for large-ensemble rehearsals and small-group lessons, as well as provide options for students to practice independently or with a partner. While these would not all be happening simultaneously, there was no way to "transform" the space multiple times each day. So it became an opportunity to think outside of the box.

She configured the chairs and music stands so they would work with each of her ensembles. When practicing independently or with a classmate, students could sit anywhere in those chairs. She also purchased four IKEA stools and stored them under a counter so students could move them anywhere in the room during group lessons. In one corner there used to be a file cabinet tucked between the instrument storage cubbies and the door. Theresa moved the cabinet and replaced it with a music stand and a sign for the "Practice Nook," which is perfect for individuals who need a little more privacy and fewer distractions when practicing. Finally, in one corner of the storage closet, Theresa created a "recording studio" where students could go to record video assignments or other creations. The studio has a music stand and chair, along with several pieces of acoustic foam on the wall. It isn't sound-proof, but it definitely affords a better recording experience.

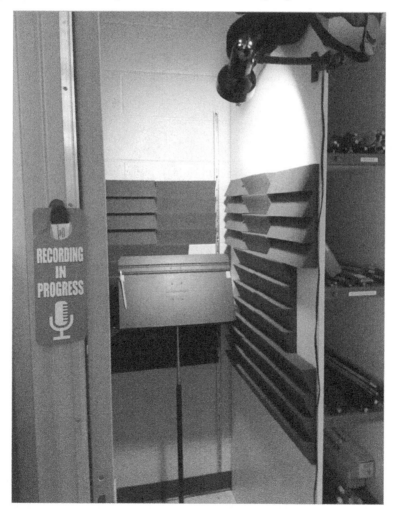

Theresa's recording studio

When looking at your space, also consider movement flow and ease of access to necessary supplies and materials. Create a space that has easy traffic flow so students can smoothly transition from one thing to another. In her classroom, Theresa also created a "Student Center" where everyone could easily access materials and supplies they might need during the class period (borrowed from Joy Kirr's book *Shift This!* which mentions a "Student Station"). The Student Center is on the counter along one wall of the classroom and contains small buckets with typical school supplies: regular and colored pencils, erasers, and scissors. There are also containers with rosin, cork grease, valve oil, mouthpiece brushes, rubber bands (for upper strings), and shoulder rests. The students understand these materials are to borrow if they've forgotten something, not to be removed from the classroom.

A Student Center with school supplies and instrument supplies

Finally, the Student Center contains file folders with extra lesson books, supplemental books, and extra copies of ensemble music. While it's true the students "should" have their own copies of everything, sometimes people forget. It happens to the best of us. They know if they borrow something from the Student Center, it's their responsibility to replace it before leaving the classroom. To date, this system has worked very well. The students respect and appreciate the items in the Student Center. Having access to it enables them to take ownership and solve problems on their own.

These changes to the space work for us and our students. You will need to think about the learning goals for your students before working on your space. This could also be a valuable time to talk to them and ask what they need. You may remember from Chapter 4, Kathryn asked students to give feedback about the classroom space. Two requests she implemented included a green screen and a recording studio, both of which get used frequently throughout the school year. She might have eventually come up with these ideas on her own, but because she had asked the students, she felt confident both additions would make an impact in the classroom. Take a chance. Ask your students what you could do to the space that would help them learn and make music most effectively. Their insight might surprise you!

Kathryn's green screen

Fine

There are so many priorities for us to think about as music educators. We are busy trying to keep up with standards, traditions, multiple classes, and a large volume of students. Sometimes it feels too hard to try something new. And yet we encourage you to take a risk. Keep pushing yourself away from comfortable. When we get too comfortable, we fall behind. We owe it to our students and ourselves to take small steps toward innovation. Our world is constantly changing, and as music teachers, we can reflect those changes in our classrooms to prepare students for an unknown future.

At this point you have finished the book, or at least skipped to the end (we'll never know)! Either way, this is where two critical things need to happen. First, take action. Try something new. Take a chance. Reading this book and then continuing to do things the same way you always have would be a disservice to your students. They deserve a change, and so do you. Know that you are not alone in this journey. Follow #PasstheBatonBook on Twitter to share and learn with other music educators dedicated to making these shifts.

As you take action, celebrate the victories, failures, and everything in between. Taking a chance and making a change in your classroom is something to be proud of, so reward yourself for your efforts. Just as we celebrate students for their victories in the classroom and also acknowledge the value of their failures, you deserve this same recognition.

The second thing to do is share this book with another music teacher. Someone who is ready to hear its message. Compare notes, share experiences—the good, the bad, and the ugly—and encourage one another to keep at it. Show your commitment not only to your own students, but to all students! Remember above all that it may not be easy—but it will be worth it.

Notes

Chapter 2

1. William M. Sloan, "What Is the Purpose of Education," *Education Update* 54, no. 7, www.ascd.org/publications/newsletters/education-update/jul12/vol54/num07/What-Is-the-Purpose-of-Education%C2%A2.aspx.
2. Michael Mark, *A Concise History of American Music Education* (United States: R&L Education, 2008).
3. National Association for Music Education, "Child's Bill of Rights," adopted November 1, 1991, nafme.org/my-classroom/journals-magazines/nafme-online-publications/childs-bill-of-rights/.
4. Bob Phillips, interview with Doug Conrad, *Directors Circle*, podcast, May 1, 2019, directorscircle.libsyn.com/bob-phillips-episode-9.

Chapter 3

1. Daniel Pink, *Drive: The Surprising Truth about what Motivates Us* (New York: Riverhead Books, 2009).

Chapter 4

1. Laurie Barron, EdD, and Patti Kinney, *Middle School: A Place to Belong and Become* (Westerville, Ohio: Associations for Middle Level Education, 2018).
2. Bena Kallick and Allison Zmuda, *Students at the Center: Personalized Learning with Habits of Mind* (Alexandria, Virginia: ASCD, 2017).
3. Barbara Bray and Kathleen McClaskey, *How to Personalize Learning: A Practical Guide for Getting Started and Going Deeper* (Thousand Oaks, California: Corwin, 2017).

Chapter 5

1. Pink, *Drive*.
2. Mike Anderson, *Learning to Choose, Choosing to Learn* (Alexandria, Virginia: ASCD, 2016).

Chapter 6

1. John Spencer and A. J. Juliani, *Empower: What Happens when Students Own Their Learning* (San Diego, California: IMPress, 2017).
2. John Mackey, "How I Spent My Teen Years," Osti Music, February 9, 2015, ostimusic.com/blog/how-i-spent-my-teen-years/.

Chapter 7

1. Heather Wolpert-Gawron, "What the Heck Is Inquiry-Based Learning?," Edutopia, August 11, 2016, www.edutopia.org/blog/what-heck-inquiry-based-learning-heather-wolpert-gawron.
2. Trevor Mackenzie and Rebecca Bathurst-Hunt, *Inquiry Mindset: Nurturing the Dreams, Wonders, and Curiosities of Our Youngest Learners*, EdTechTeam Press, 2018.

3. 3M, "Life with 3M," www.3m.com/3M/en_US/careers-us/working-at-3m/life -with-3m/.
4. A. J. Juliani, "What Is Genius Hour?," Genius Hour, geniushour.com/what-is -genius-hour/.
5. Warren Berger, "How Brainstorming Questions, Not Ideas, Sparks Creativity,"*Fast Company*, June 6, 2016, www.fastcompany.com/3060573/ how-brainstorming-questions-not-ideas-sparks-creativity.
6. Tomas Chamorro-Premuzic, "Curiosity Is as Important as Intelligence," *Harvard Business Review*, August 27, 2014, hbr.org/2014/08/curiosity-is-as -important-as-intelligence.

Chapter 8
1. Daniel Goleman, "What Makes a Leader," *Harvard Business Review*, January 2004, hbr.org/2004/01/what-makes-a-leader.
2. Rushton Hurley, "Home," accessed September 30, 2020, rushtonh.com/ home.
3. School Ensemble Recording Exchange, sites.google.com/bvsd.org/ ensemblerecordingexchange/home.

Chapter 9
1. PBLWorks, "What Is PBL?," www.pblworks.org/what-is-pbl.
2. Shenandoah University News, "Growing a Musical," May 24, 2019, www.su .edu/blog/2019/05/growing-a-musical/.
3. Shenandoah University News, "Student Performance Week Project by Barricklo '21 Approved for Use in NICU at Winchester Medical Center," March 19, 2019, www.su.edu/blog/2019/03/student-performance-week-project-by -barricklo-21-approved-for-use-in-nicu-at-winchester-medical-center/.

Chapter 10
1. Steve Giddings, "5 Reasons for Starting a Rock Band at Your School (Part 1)," Steve's Music Room, August 19, 2017, stevesmusicroom. wordpress. com/2017/08/19/5-reasons-for-starting-a-rock-band-at-your -school.

Chapter 11
1. Ryan [Barone], "Coding for Kids: Reasons Kids Should Get Started, and how They Can Find Succes," iDTech, September 18, 2019, www.idtech.com/ blog/5-reasons-your-child-should-learn-to-code.
2. Semi-Conductor, semiconductor.withgoogle.com/.
3. Jay Allen Zimmerman, "Seeing Music," Experiments with Google, October 2018, experiments.withgoogle.com/seeing-music.
4. NYU Music Experience Design Lab, "Groove Pizza," July 2016, experiments. withgoogle.com/groove-pizza.
5. Holly Clark and Tanya Avrith, *The Google Infused Classroom* (EdTechTeamPress, 2017).

Chapter 12

1. Diane DeMott Painter, "Teacher Research Could Change Your Practice," NEA, accessed August 19, 2019, ftp.arizonaea.org/tools/17289.htm.

2. National Association for Music Education, "Strategic Plan," adopted on October 23, 2015, nafme.org/wp-content/files/2014/06/Strategic-Plan_ revised-2016.pdf.

3. National Association for Music Education, "NAfME Research," accessed September 30, 2020, nafme.org/nafme-research/.

About the Authors

Kathryn Finch

Kathryn Finch has twenty-two years of experience in the elementary general music classroom and currently teaches in a northern suburb of Chicago. She speaks passionately about the shift in music education from teacher-led activities to student-led activities and focuses on practical ways music educators can transform their classrooms to empower their students to own their learning.

She has been a guest on the *Music Ed Mentor* podcast on empowering music students, and recently joined the team at *Activate!* magazine as a contributing author of general music lesson plans. A published work of Kathryn's, *Creating Adaptive Instruments with a Makey Makey*, can be found in the fall 2019 issue of the *Illinois Music Educator Journal* as she is also passionate about an inclusive music experience for all her students. Kathryn has coauthored two teaching resources, *Full STEAM Ahead: Lessons to Shift Instruction, Empower Students, and Transform Your Music Classroom* and *Everyone Loves a Story: Bringing Books to Life through Music*. You can read about Kathryn's professional journey at www.ponderingsfromafinch.com.

Kathryn received her bachelor's degree in music education from Augustana College and her master's in music education from VanderCook College of Music. She is a cocreator of the #BlairFinchProject, certified in all three levels of Orff Schulwerk, an Apple Teacher, and serves as a technology leader in her school district.

Kathryn lives near Chicago, Illinois, with her husband, two children, an energetic Brittany spaniel, and an emotionally challenged Chihuahua. If she isn't writing, Kathryn is taking walks with the dogs, experimenting in the kitchen, or creating sewing projects with her family to support local organizations.

Bring Kathryn Finch to Your School or Event

Kathryn Finch shares her personal experience and passion in her workshops and professional development sessions. Teachers will be inspired to innovate and have practical next steps to build and grow on. Presentations can be in person or in a virtual setting.

Popular Messages from Kathryn Finch

Kathryn feels passionately about empowering students in the music classroom and challenges us as music educators to shift our instruction and technology integration to a learner-centered approach. As each school or event is unique, Kathryn's presentations can be customized to meet the needs of her participants. Possible topics may include:

- ♪ Go Beyond Student Engagement . . . to Empowerment!
- ♪ Full STEAM Ahead: Lessons to Shift Instruction, Empower Students, and Transform Your Music Classroom
- ♪ Learning First, Technology Second
- ♪ Everyone Loves a Story: Bringing Books to Life through Music

Connect with Kathryn Finch

Connect with Kathryn Finch for more information about bringing her to your event.

- ♪ Twitter: @Singingfinch1
- ♪ Email: kathryn@passthebatonbook.com
- ♪ Blog: ponderingsfromafinch.com

Theresa Hoover

Theresa Hoover is a music educator, speaker, and writer. She is an advocate for student voice in the music room and works to empower students throughout their musical experiences while helping teachers transform their classrooms into student-centered learning environments.

Currently Theresa teaches middle school band in Northern Virginia, having opened a brand-new middle school in 2019. Prior to moving to Virginia in 2016, she taught instrumental, general, and vocal music in a variety of settings in Pennsylvania for thirteen years. She holds a bachelor's degree in music education from Penn State University and a master's degree in wind conducting from West Chester University, also in Pennsylvania.

Theresa is a recognized presenter and clinician at conferences at the local, regional, and national level, including the International Music Education Summit, the Virginia Society for Technology in Education conference, and several state music education conferences. She is a Google for Education Certified Trainer and was selected as a member of the Google Certified Innovator program, participating in the London 2019 cohort.

In addition to her schoolteaching, Theresa was the founding director of the Chester County Youth Wind Ensemble and currently serves on the staff of the Virginia Winds Academy. She has also been the guest conductor for several elementary and middle school ensembles in Pennsylvania and Virginia.

When not teaching, Theresa can be found curled up with a good book, on the running trail, traveling to visit family and friends, or spending time with her dog, Dizzy.

Bring Theresa Hoover to Your School or Event

Theresa Hoover brings her passion and enthusiasm to presentations, workshops, and professional development programs in both in-person and virtual settings. Her sessions are inspiring and practical. Teachers will leave not only excited to try new things in their classrooms, but also with a clear picture of how to do so.

Popular Messages from Theresa Hoover

Theresa often speaks to music educators about empowering their students, creating a learner-centered environment, and integrating technology into the music room. Theresa's presentations can be customized to meet the unique needs of your event. Here are some of the keynote presentations she has done in the past:

- ♪ Maximize Student Voice and Choice in Music
- ♪ Go Beyond Student Engagement . . . to Empowerment!
- ♪ Let's Get Googley: Tips for the Google-Filled Music Room
- ♪ You Can't Pour from an Empty Cup: Practical Tips for Music Teacher Well-Being

Connect

Connect with Theresa Hoover for more information about bringing her to your event.

- ♪ Twitter and Instagram: @MusicalTheresa
- ♪ Email: theresa@passthebatonbook.com
- ♪ Blog: www.offthebeatenpathinmusic.com

More from

Since 2012, DBCI has published books that inspire and equip educators to be their best. For more information on our titles or to purchase bulk orders for your school, district, or book study, visit **DaveBurgessConsulting.com/DBCIbooks**.

More Teaching Methods & Materials

All 4s and 5s by Andrew Sharos

Boredom Busters by Katie Powell

The Classroom Chef by John Stevens and Matt Vaudrey

The Collaborative Classroom by Trevor Muir

Copyrighteous by Diana Gill

CREATE by Bethany J. Petty

Ditch That Homework by Matt Miller and Alice Keeler

Ditch That Textbook by Matt Miller

Don't Ditch That Tech by Matt Miller, Nate Ridgway, and
    Angelia Ridgway

EDrenaline Rush by John Meehan

Educated by Design by Michael Cohen, The Tech Rabbi

The EduProtocol Field Guide by Marlena Hebern and Jon Corippo

The EduProtocol Field Guide: Book 2 by Marlena Hebern and
    Jon Corippo

Instant Relevance by Denis Sheeran

LAUNCH by John Spencer and A.J. Juliani

Make Learning MAGICAL by Tisha Richmond

Pure Genius by Don Wettrick

The Revolution by Darren Ellwein and Derek McCoy

Shift This! by Joy Kirr

Skyrocket Your Teacher Coaching by Michael Cary Sonbert

Spark Learning by Ramsey Musallam

Sparks in the Dark by Travis Crowder and Todd Nesloney
Table Talk Math by John Stevens
The Wild Card by Hope and Wade King
The Writing on the Classroom Wall by Steve Wyborney

Like a PIRATE™ Series

Teach Like a PIRATE by Dave Burgess
eXPlore Like a Pirate by Michael Matera
Learn Like a Pirate by Paul Solarz
Play Like a Pirate by Quinn Rollins
Run Like a Pirate by Adam Welcome
Tech Like a PIRATE by Matt Miller

Lead Like a PIRATE™ Series

Lead Like a PIRATE by Shelley Burgess and Beth Houf
Balance Like a Pirate by Jessica Cabeen, Jessica Johnson, and
    Sarah Johnson
Lead beyond Your Title by Nili Bartley
Lead with Appreciation by Amber Teamann and Melinda Miller
Lead with Culture by Jay Billy
Lead with Instructional Rounds by Vicki Wilson
Lead with Literacy by Mandy Ellis

Leadership & School Culture

Culturize by Jimmy Casas
Escaping the School Leader's Dunk Tank by Rebecca Coda and
    Rick Jetter
Fight Song by Kim Bearden
From Teacher to Leader by Starr Sackstein
If the Dance Floor Is Empty, Change the Song by Joe Clark
The Innovator's Mindset by George Couros
It's OK to Say "They" by Christy Whittlesey
Kids Deserve It! by Todd Nesloney and Adam Welcome
Let Them Speak by Rebecca Coda and Rick Jetter
The Limitless School by Abe Hege and Adam Dovico

Live Your Excellence by Jimmy Casas

Next-Level Teaching by Jonathan Alsheimer

The Pepper Effect by Sean Gaillard

The Principled Principal by Jeffrey Zoul and Anthony McConnell

Relentless by Hamish Brewer

The Secret Solution by Todd Whitaker, Sam Miller, and Ryan Donlan

Start. Right. Now. by Todd Whitaker, Jeffrey Zoul, and Jimmy Casas

Stop. Right. Now. by Jimmy Casas and Jeffrey Zoul

Teachers Deserve It by Rae Hughart and Adam Welcome

Teach Your Class Off by CJ Reynolds

They Call Me "Mr. De" by Frank DeAngelis

Thrive through the Five by Jill M. Siler

Unmapped Potential by Julie Hasson and Missy Lennard

When Kids Lead by Todd Nesloney and Adam Dovico

Word Shift by Joy Kirr

Your School Rocks by Ryan McLane and Eric Lowe

Technology & Tools

50 Things You Can Do with Google Classroom by Alice Keeler and Libbi Miller

50 Things to Go Further with Google Classroom by Alice Keeler and Libbi Miller

140 Twitter Tips for Educators by Brad Currie, Billy Krakower, and Scott Rocco

Block Breaker by Brian Aspinall

Code Breaker by Brian Aspinall

Control Alt Achieve by Eric Curts

Google Apps for Littles by Christine Pinto and Alice Keeler

Master the Media by Julie Smith

Reality Bytes by Christine Lion-Bailey, Jesse Lubinsky, and Micah Shippee, PhD

Sail the 7 Cs with Microsoft Education by Becky Keene and Kathi Kersznowski

Shake Up Learning by Kasey Bell

Social LEADia by Jennifer Casa-Todd

Stepping Up to Google Classroom by Alice Keeler and Kimberly Mattina

Teaching Math with Google Apps by Alice Keeler and Diana Herrington

Teachingland by Amanda Fox and Mary Ellen Weeks

Inspiration, Professional Growth & Personal Development

Be REAL by Tara Martin

Be the One for Kids by Ryan Sheehy

The Coach ADVenture by Amy Illingworth

Creatively Productive by Lisa Johnson

Educational Eye Exam by Alicia Ray

The EduNinja Mindset by Jennifer Burdis

Empower Our Girls by Lynmara Colón and Adam Welcome

Finding Lifelines by Andrew Grieve and Andrew Sharos

The Four O'Clock Faculty by Rich Czyz

How Much Water Do We Have? by Pete and Kris Nunweiler

P Is for Pirate by Dave and Shelley Burgess

A Passion for Kindness by Tamara Letter

The Path to Serendipity by Allyson Apsey

Sanctuaries by Dan Tricarico

The SECRET SAUCE by Rich Czyz

Shattering the Perfect Teacher Myth by Aaron Hogan

Stories from Webb by Todd Nesloney

Talk to Me by Kim Bearden

Teach Better by Chad Ostrowski, Tiffany Ott, Rae Hughart, and Jeff Gargas

Teach Me, Teacher by Jacob Chastain

Teach, Play, Learn! by Adam Peterson

The Teachers of Oz by Herbie Raad and Nathan Lang-Raad

TeamMakers by Laura Robb and Evan Robb

Through the Lens of Serendipity by Allyson Apsey

The Zen Teacher by Dan Tricarico

Children's Books

Beyond Us by Aaron Polansky

Cannonball In by Tara Martin

Dolphins in Trees by Aaron Polansky

I Want to Be a Lot by Ashley Savage

The Princes of Serendip by Allyson Apsey

The Wild Card Kids by Hope and Wade King

Zom-Be a Design Thinker by Amanda Fox

Made in the USA
Monee, IL
02 November 2020

46559809R00125